# The Acculturation Experiences of ELLs Within the Classroom Learning Environment in the United States

# The Acculturation Experiences of ELLs Within the Classroom Learning Environment in the United States

Dissertation Manuscript

Submitted to National University
JFK School of Psychology & Social Sciences
in Partial Fulfillment of the
Requirements for the Degree of
DOCTOR OF PHILOSOPHY

by
EDNER PIERREVIL

San Diego, California
July 2024

# Contents

## ABSTRACT

This qualitative, descriptive phenomenological study explored the acculturation experiences of English Language Learners (ELLs) within the classroom learning environment in the United States. The problem addressed in this study was the acculturation experiences of ELLs within the classroom learning environment in the United States. The purpose of this study was to explore the acculturation experiences of ELLs within the classroom learning environment in the United States. Berry's acculturation theory was used as the theoretical framework for the study. Giorgi's descriptive phenomenological design was used to guide the data analysis process of this study. Purposive sampling was used, and data saturation was reached after collecting data from eight participants. The participants were public elementary school teachers in the Southeastern United States. The member-checking process was used to ensure the accuracy of the semi-structured interview transcriptions represented by the participants' descriptions of the phenomenon. Then, Giorgi's five-step data analysis techniques were applied. After that, nine constituents emerged in response to three research questions in the study. The results of the study are supported by the current studies. The potential implications and recommendations for future research were included in the study.

## ACKNOWLEDGMENTS

This accomplishment is dedicated to God. As stated in Psalm 113:7-8, "He raises the poor from the dust and lifts the needy from the ash heap; He seats them with princes, with the princes of His people." Additionally, Philippians 4:13 affirms, "I can do all this through Him who gives me strength." Psalm 40:17 expresses, "But as for me, I am poor and needy; may the Lord think of me. You are my help and my deliverer; You are my God; do not delay." Finally, Psalm 150:1-6 proclaims, "Praise the LORD. Praise God in His sanctuary; praise Him in His mighty heavens. Praise Him for His acts of power; praise Him for His surpassing greatness. Praise Him with the sounding of the trumpet, praise Him with the harp and lyre, praise Him with timbrel and dancing, praise Him with the strings and pipe, praise Him with the clash of cymbals, praise Him with resounding cymbals. Let everything that has breath praise the LORD. Praise the LORD."

I extend my gratitude and acknowledgments to my Chair, Dr. Daimon Verace, my Subject Matter Expert, Dr. Joel Goodin, and my Academic Reader, Dr. Madia Levin, for their invaluable feedback during my doctoral dissertation journey. I also acknowledge Dr. Vardine Simeus, Dr. Charlene Desir, and doctoral candidate Rev. Jean Yves Marcelon for their encouragement and support throughout this long journey.

I am grateful to my daughters, Limene Pierrevil, Edna Pierrevil, Kathrine Pierrevil, Ruth Pierrevil, and my son, Luther Philippe Pierrevil, for their unwavering support. I acknowledge my father, Pierrevilus Pierrevil, for his initial investment.

I also extend my gratitude to my pastor, Rev. Jean Smith Soiro, and the members of Mount Olives Church for their prayers. Additionally, I thank my dear friend, Rev. Pastor Cidieu Augustin, who first gave me a teaching job.

Finally, I express my deepest appreciation to my distinguished wife, Neslie Immacula St. Fleur Pierrevil, whose essential support made this achievement possible.

This study explored the acculturation experiences of English language learners (ELLs) within the classroom learning environment in the United States. ELLs face significant challenges in the school setting (Garcia-Borrego et al., 2020). They come from various countries, and English is not their primary language (Garcia-Borrego et al., 2020; Watkinson et al., 2022). The population of ELLs is the fastest-growing group of students in the United States, spanning elementary, middle, and high school settings (Gilblom et al., 2022; Shim & Shur, 2018; Watkinson et al., 2022). Over the past decade, the ELL population in the United States has increased rapidly (Zhang et al., 2022). Johnson and Thorne-Wallington (2021) found that the student population in the United States has become more diverse.

The population of ELLs in the public schools in the United States was about 5 million students in 2000 (Zhang et al., 2022). Globalization and the current wave of immigrants have increased the population of ELLs in the United States (Szymanski & Lynch, 2020). Also, by 2025, one in four students in the United States will be an ELL (Shim & Shur, 2018). In addition, researchers stated that ELLs face tremendous challenges as students in the United States (Ma & Xia, 2021; Watkinson et al., 2022). The challenges faced by ELLs include the poor acculturation experiences of assimilating to the new school culture environment, challenges of learning the English language, and lower academic achievement (Stark et al., 2021; Watkinson et al., 2022).

ELLs often face acculturation experiences, such as difficulties assimilating to a new, culturally welcoming classroom environment (Parker et al., 2021; Stark et al., 2021). Researchers have defined acculturation as an acquisition of a new culture and assimilation to the new culture changes (Parker et al., 2021; Yingling, 2023). For example, studies have shown that acculturation may be challenging in building social relationships within the classroom (Parker et al., 2021; Stark et al., 2021). Also, some other acculturation challenges and experiences ELLs face include limited English proficiency, social communication skills, social isolation, and loneliness (Stark et al., 2021; Yingling, 2023). The acculturation experiences often manifest as worry, fear, embarrassment, frustration, and anxiety in the new classroom learning environment (Parker et al., 2021). For instance, studies revealed that acculturation experiences increase stress on ELLs as they try to integrate into their new classroom cultural learning environment (Gilblom et al., 2022; Parker et al., 2021). Such experiences have interfered with ELLs' motivation to engage in their classroom interaction activities (Parker et al., 2021). Additionally, ELLs suffer from cultural exclusion and face cultural disadvantages in their classroom (Wang & Yu, 2021). Researchers have advocated for socioculturally relevant and inclusive classrooms for ELLs in the U.S. education system (Stark et al., 2021; Wang & Yu, 2021).

The acculturation experiences and challenges faced by ELLs are not without consequences (Dessie & Sewagegn, 2019; Kraus, 2023). The acculturation experiences and challenges ELLs face within their classroom have learning and academic implications (Gilblom et al., 2022; Ma & Xia, 2021; Stark et al., 2021). Researchers have stated that there is a direct relationship between acculturation experiences and adaptation to a new culture learning environment (Stark et al., 2021; Watkinson et al., 2022). For instance, acculturation experiences and acculturative stress have significantly impacted ELLs' abilities and contributed to more English language deficiency, increased language barriers, and resulted in negative academic consequences (Gilblom et al., 2022; Ma & Xia, 2021). According to Fang (2020), the experiences of acculturation require new attitudes. Researchers have found that positive attitudes toward the new cultural environment increase the academic achievement of the learners (Fang, 2020; Gilblom et al., 2022; Stark et al., 2021). Therefore, positive acculturation experiences are essential for improving the academic achievement of ELLs (Fang, 2020). Also, cultural inclusion in a classroom environment is critical to assimilation, improving academic performance, and reducing the poor acculturation experiences and stigma of ELLs (Gilblom et al., 2022; Parker et al., 2021; Stark et al., 2021). On the other hand, researchers have stated that unfavorable and negative acculturation experiences have contributed to more social-emotional and behavioral challenges and lower academic achievement among learners (Fang, 2020; Wang & Yu, 2021; Zhang et al., 2022).

The population of ELLs faces many challenges (Zhang et al., 2022). These challenges faced by ELLs include new classroom learning environments, English language deficiency issues, academic risk, classification as the lower academic achievement group, and lower graduation rates among students in public school settings (Johnson & Thorne-Wallington, 2021; Wang & Yu, 2021; Zhang et al., 2022). The population of ELLs has faced tremendous challenges and exceptional achievement risks (Fang, 2020; Stark et al., 2021). The academic achievements of ELLs are more problematic and alarming compared to other groups of students (Murphy & Torff, 2019).

The academic performance of English Language Learners (ELLs) is a significant issue. For instance, the dropout rates among ELLs are higher than those of their peers (Fang, 2020; Gilblom et al., 2022; Shim & Shur, 2018). Researchers have reported that the graduation rate in Virginia is about 92% among mainstream students, while the graduation rate among ELLs is 82% (Owens & Wells, 2021). Additionally, ELLs lag by 30–40 points on state assessments (Olds et al., 2021). On average, ELLs perform below their grade level (Soland & Sandilos, 2021) and score 31% to 33% lower than other students (Cho et al., 2022).

The challenges faced by ELLs have increased the need for a culturally relevant classroom learning environment to meet their needs in the United States (Cho et al., 2019; Dessie & Sewagegn, 2019). Studies have found that teachers' perspectives and roles are critical in supporting ELLs' experiences (Cho et al., 2019; Dessie & Sewagegn, 2019; Saito et al., 2018). Saito et al. (2018) claimed that teachers significantly influence the acculturation experiences and academic achievement of ELLs. Researchers suggest that teachers can create cultural classroom environments conducive to meeting the needs of their ELL students (Hong et al., 2019). For instance, teachers need to have appropriate and relevant cultural expectations regarding their ELL students (Cho et al., 2019; Dessie & Sewagegn, 2019). Studies revealed that ELLs tend to be embarrassed and reluctant to participate in classroom discussions when the environment is not conducive to their new learning experiences

(Davis & Tesh, 2022). Therefore, acculturation experiences, limited English proficiency, and challenges in assimilating to the new school culture have created significant disadvantages, labeling ELLs as the nation's lowest academic-performing group of students (Cho et al., 2019; Hong et al., 2019; Stark et al., 2021; Wang & Yu, 2021; Zhang et al., 2022).

## Statement of the Problem

The problem addressed in this study was the acculturation experiences of ELLs within the classroom learning environment in the United States (Bennouna et al., 2021; Hendy & Cuevas, 2020; Hong et al., 2019; Murray, 2020; Soland & Sandilos, 2021). Studies have revealed that ELLs often experience acculturation challenges in integrating into the new cultural classroom learning environment (Al-Krenawi et al., 2021; Bowers et al., 2022; Hieu, 2023). The literature review on ELLs demonstrates that the acculturation experiences of the ELL population can take several forms, such as language barriers and a limited ability to socialize in the classroom environment (Bennouna et al., 2021; Hieu, 2023; Meng, 2020). For example, ELLs with limited English language proficiency often experience peer rejection (Meng, 2020). Also, researchers have indicated that English language proficiency is an essential factor in the acculturation experience and a vehicle for acquiring classroom cultural knowledge and academic achievement in the United States (Zaidi et al., 2021). For instance, the lack of English language proficiency makes the experiences of ELLs more difficult as they learn the classroom curriculum, meet their grade-level requirements, and socially integrate into their classroom learning environment (Bennouna et al., 2021; Hieu, 2023).

The unfavorable acculturation experiences of ELLs lead to poorer academic performance (Boileau et al., 2022). ELLs often experience challenges in achieving academic success in the core content areas (Soland & Sandilos, 2021). For example, ELLs who lack English language proficiency face challenges in passing the state exams and have limited motivation to assimilate to the new cultural learning experiences (Hong et al., 2019; Soland & Sandilos, 2021). Researchers have indicated that such acculturation experiences often lead to psychosocial issues that impact academic performance, increase the risk of dropping out of school, and negatively shape the graduation rates of the ELL population in the United States (Bennouna et al., 2021; Hieu, 2023; Murray, 2020; Soland & Sandilos, 2021).

## Purpose of the Study

The purpose of this qualitative, descriptive phenomenological study was to explore the acculturation experiences of ELLs within the classroom learning environment in the United States. A descriptive phenomenological design was essential to understanding and interpreting the meaning and essence of the individuals' lived experiences (Giorgi, 2009). The study explored the acculturation experiences of ELLs within the classroom learning environment through teachers who have experience working with ELLs in the Southeastern United States. The public school teachers were selected and recruited to participate in the study instead of ELLs directly because many ELLs did not have enough English language proficiency to share their own experiences. The data were collected by using semi-structured interviews. An interview guide was used during the interview process. According to Giorgi (2009), a sample size is difficult to consider and pre-determine. However, the data saturation process was used to ensure and provide a meaningful description of the phenomenon of the study. Giorgi (2009) suggested that researchers can recruit more participants until data saturation is reached. Ten teachers were recruited to participate in this study. Researchers are allowed to recruit more participants to continue with the interview if the saturation is not met with the proposed participants in the study (Hennink & Kaiser, 2022). Saturation in qualitative studies is an important factor (Hennink & Kaiser, 2022; Vasileiou et al., 2018). For example, saturation is the end goal; it is where the data cannot provide any new concepts from the interviews (Hennink & Kaiser, 2022; Vasileiou et al., 2018). Researchers stated that saturation can be considered the end of the data analysis process (Fofana et al., 2020; Vasileiou et al., 2018). Also, researchers claimed that saturation is where the data could not generate any new information for the research questions (Fofana et al., 2020; Vasileiou et al., 2018). However, eight participants were included in this qualitative descriptive phenomenological study. The participants provided a meaningful understanding of the lived experiences of ELLs within the classroom learning environment.

The study's data were analyzed using Amadeo Giorgi's (2009) five-step analysis process, which focuses on understanding human experiences. Giorgi's (2009) five-step data analysis is an essential process for gaining meaningful descriptions of the essence of the acculturation experiences of ELLs, which is the phenomenon of the study. Giorgi's (2009) five-step data analysis process includes familiarizing with all data, delineating meaning units, transforming the units into expressions of meanings lived by the participants, crafting the informed meaning structure, and the constituents emerging to generate the essential structure of the phenomenon.

## Introduction to the Theoretical Framework

Acculturation theory was used to explore the acculturation experiences of ELLs within the classroom learning environment in the United States. Acculturation theory is used to explore the lived experiences of ELLs within the classroom experiences in the United States (Antoniadou & Quinlan, 2020). Acculturation theory is a cross-cultural psychological theoretical framework used to understand how individuals interact between two cultures (Berry, 1997, 2005). Acculturation theory has been used to explore the cultural and psychological changes that follow interactions and experiences individuals encounter between the host culture, the primary cultural backgrounds, and cultural values (Berry, 2015). The aim of using acculturation theory is to show that environmental connections and interactions influence an individual's identity, attitudes, and behaviors (Berry, 1997).

Berry's (1997) acculturation theory framework includes acculturative strategies for individuals to successfully acculturate and integrate into a new cultural environment. According to Berry's (1997) acculturation theory, individuals often face acculturative stress due to unfamiliar cultures, social systems, and language barriers. The acculturation theoretical framework highlights four different strategies of acculturation: assimilation, separation, integration, and marginalization (Berry, 1997). For instance, assimilation is when individuals adopt a positive attitude toward the new culture (Berry, 1997). Separation is the strategy that indicates individuals maintain a positive attitude toward the primary culture (Berry, 1997). The integration strategy occurs when immigrants keep a positive attitude toward the new culture and their primary culture (Berry, 1997). Integration is the most positive strategy for immigrants (Berry, 1997). The marginalization strategy occurs when immigrants develop a negative attitude toward the new culture and their primary culture (Berry, 1997). The marginalization strategy leads to unhealthy attitudes that are associated with poor psychological experiences (Berry, 1997). Therefore, providing a social network and opportunities for immigrants to develop relationships with others is vital for successful acculturation experiences (Berry, 1997). However, Berry suggested that the integration process may take time, and each individual may deal with the acculturation process differently (Berry, 1997).

Berry's (1997) acculturation theory was used to explore the acculturation experiences of the ELLs. This theory provides four strategies. For instance, separation and marginalization strategies negatively impact immigrants (Berry, 1997). On the other hand, successful assimilation and integration contribute to more remarkable academic outcomes for the population of immigrants (Berry, 1997). The acculturation theoretical framework advances the principle that immigrants or ELLs can acculturate within the new cultural classroom learning environment without having a negative perception of their primary culture and values (Berry, 1997). Berry's (1997) acculturation theory provides many avenues that support the acculturation process. The avenues include understanding immigrants' history, cultural changes, language barriers, attitudes, and behavior of individuals toward the new environment (Berry, 1997).

In addition, acculturation theory explores sociocultural learning, cultural knowledge, skills, community interaction, and support for immigrants or ELLs' needs for a successful transition (Berry, 1997). Therefore, successful assimilation and integration experiences are essential to help ELLs expand their learning abilities (Dang et al., 2022; Sousa et al., 2019). Integration is critical for classroom interactions and a significant factor in helping ELLs overcome their acculturation challenges and increase their classroom integration experiences (Mardian & Nafissi, 2022). Acculturation theory has meaningful implications for providing instructional strategies that can be used to support the acculturation experiences of ELLs (Olds et al., 2021). Acculturation theory offers foundational guidelines to address the acculturation experiences of ELLs by creating a culturally sensitive classroom environment that embraces diverse experiences (Mardian & Nafissi, 2022; Olds et al., 2021). Also, the acculturation theory framework provides the most effective strategies that include teaching practices, cultural engagement, home language encouragement, cultural and instructional practices that facilitate learning, collaborative classroom discussions regarding cultural diversity, and concepts that can be used to decrease the poor acculturation experiences of the ELLs (Dang et al., 2022).

## Introduction to Research Methodology and Design (Nature of the Study)

The qualitative research design for this study was phenomenological. A qualitative method was a unique avenue to explore the in-depth lived experiences of a population (Creswell, 2013, 2014). A qualitative method is appropriate for exploring human phenomena (Creswell & Cage, 2019). Also, a qualitative method is the primary approach to truthfully exploring and providing an accurate summation of the phenomenon of the study (Creswell & Cage, 2019). The usefulness of the qualitative method is appropriate to succinct the experiences of individuals, groups of people, and organizations in a natural setting (Creswell & Cage, 2019).

A descriptive phenomenological design is used when the purpose of the study is to describe a phenomenon and provide meaningful descriptions of the participants' lived experiences (Giorgi, 2009). For instance, Giorgi (2009) indicated that a descriptive phenomenological design is the essence and psychological approach to explaining and interpreting the individual's lived experience. A descriptive phenomenological design is appropriate to identify the meaning, assess the significance of the meaning, synthesize the meaning, and present the participants' experiences of the study (Giorgi, 2009). A descriptive phenomenological design is selected when the aim of the study is to understand human lived experiences (Giorgi, 2009). A descriptive phenomenological design permits researchers to understand the participants' lived experiences by using the participants' own words and interpretations of the phenomenon (Giorgi, 2009).

Furthermore, a qualitative descriptive phenomenological design allows researchers to use several data collection approaches and techniques, such as semi-structured interviews, questionnaires, and observations (Giorgi, 2009). This qualitative descriptive phenomenological study collected data through semi-structured interviews and a demographic questionnaire. The participants of this qualitative descriptive phenomenological study were public school teachers. The purposive sample, inclusion, and exclusion criteria were considered during the process of recruiting participants for this study. Therefore, eight elementary school teachers participated in this study. Giorgi's (2009) data analysis process was the appropriate strategy for data analysis in this study. The descriptive phenomenological analysis technique provided a meaningful way to describe the lived experience of the participants (Giorgi, 2009). For instance, the aim of Giorgi's (2009) five-step data analysis is to identify the meaning, assess the significance of the meaning, synthesize the meaning, and present the experiences of the participants of the study.

A qualitative descriptive phenomenological study was appropriate to address the problem of this study, which was the acculturation experiences of ELLs within the classroom learning environment in the United States. Researchers stated that ELLs face acculturation obstacles and academic challenges (Danford, 2023; Karimi et al., 2020; O'Brien et al., 2019). Therefore, by exploring the acculturation experiences faced by ELLs within the classroom learning environment in the United States, especially from teachers' perspectives, the study's results may provide greater awareness to the school district, school administrators, teachers, and others of the problems and challenges faced by ELLs within the classroom learning environment in the United States. Then, they may take steps forward and make effective decisions to help ELLs overcome their acculturation experiences and improve their academic achievement. Overcoming the challenges is essential and significant for the population of ELLs in the United States. A qualitative descriptive phenomenological study was appropriate to explore the research questions of this study. The following research questions were used to address the problem of this study.

## Research Questions

### *RQ1*

What are teachers' lived experiences of the acculturation faced by ELLs within the classroom learning environment in the United States?

### *RQ2*

What are teachers' lived experiences addressing the acculturation of ELLs within the classroom learning environment in the United States?

### *RQ3*

What are the strategies that teachers use to address the acculturation experiences of ELLs within the classroom learning environment in the United States?

## Significance of the Study

This study was significant because the results may contribute to improving the acculturation experiences of ELLs within the classroom learning environment in the United States. The study's results may provide school administrators with greater awareness of ELLs' acculturation experiences in the classroom. Also, the study results may help ELLs overcome their academic challenges, which are essential and vital for the ELL population in the United States. The findings of the study may help teachers and school administrators develop more effective coping strategies to support ELLs with their acculturation experiences, assimilate into the new cultural classroom learning environment, support ELLs in overcoming their academic challenges, and help ELLs achieve greater academic performance in the United States as a minority group of students (Parker et al., 2021; Stark et al., 2021). For instance, the contribution of this study may enhance and improve teachers' and school administrators' perceptions regarding the effective strategies they can use to mitigate the poor acculturation experiences faced by ELLs in the United States. Also,

Berry's (1997) acculturation theory may not fully apply to explore the ELLs who live in the Southeastern United States yet. Therefore, this study provided a better understanding of how Berry's (1997) acculturation theory may be applied and used to fully understand the lived experiences of all ELL groups in the United States.

The study's results contribute to the current literature on understanding the acculturation experiences of ELLs within the classroom and their academic performance. I hope that the results of the study might influence school stakeholders' decisions by creating a cultural classroom learning environment and classroom curriculum by providing social network activities and coping strategies to support ELLs. Then, the ELL population may be able to overcome their acculturation experiences and educational barriers, learn the English language more effectively, and close their overdue achievement gap. Finally, the study was significant because it focused on the problem, the purpose, and the research questions of the study, which addressed the acculturation experiences of ELLs within the classroom learning environment that affected their academic achievement in the United States as students.

## Definitions of Key Terms

### Academic Achievement

Academic achievement is defined as the intellectual domains in which an individual has accomplished specific academic goals (Mašková & Kučera, 2022).

### Acculturation

Acculturation is defined as the acquisition of a new culture and assimilation to the new changes (Parker et al., 2021; Yingling, 2023).

### Acculturative stress

Acculturative stress is related to the general individual processing of life experiences that are linked to the process of acculturation (Pacheco, 2020).

### Assimilation

Assimilation is referred to when an individual does not maintain their culture but adapts to the main culture (Krsmanovic, 2020).

### Classroom Learning

Classroom learning is a creative and critical environment that influences the students' academic achievement (Noor et al., 2021).

### English Language Learners (ELLs)

English language learners (ELLs) are students for whom the English language is not their first language (Garcia-Borrego et al., 2020; Watkinson et al., 2022).

### Learning Environment

A learning environment is a conducive classroom learning environment that directly affects students' learning and development (Cai et al., 2022).

## Summary

The aim of Chapter 1 was to establish a foundation for this study. The problem addressed in this study was the acculturation experiences of ELLs within the classroom learning environment in the United States (Bennouna et al., 2021; Hong et al., 2019; Murray, 2020; Soland & Sandilos, 2021). The purpose of this qualitative, descriptive phenomenological study was to explore the acculturation experiences of ELLs within the classroom learning environment in the United States from teachers' perspectives. This study was guided by Berry's (1997) acculturation theory. Berry's (1997) acculturation theory was used to address the lived experiences of ELLs within the classroom. Semi-structured interviews were conducted with public elementary school teachers. The data were analyzed using Giorgi's (2009) five-step data process. This study was significant because the findings may enhance ELLs' acculturation experiences and improve their academic achievement as the most vulnerable students in the United States. Chapter 2 provides more detail on the literature review regarding ELLs' acculturation and academic experiences in the United States.

The purpose of this qualitative, descriptive phenomenological study was to explore the lived experiences of the population of ELLs as they try to acculturate within the classroom learning environment in the United States. Specifically, the acculturation experiences of ELLs significantly impacted their classroom learning achievement (Bennouna et al., 2021; Hendy & Cuevas, 2020; Hong et al., 2019; Murray, 2020; Soland & Sandilos, 2021). Exploring the acculturation experiences of ELLs was essential to understanding the challenges they face within the classroom learning environment as a growing group of students in the United States (Hendy & Cuevas, 2020). The qualitative, descriptive phenomenological method provides a unique avenue to fully comprehend, describe, and interpret individuals' lived experiences (Giorgi, 2009). In this chapter, the researcher analyzes and synthesizes a literature review of research studies related to the acculturation experiences of ELLs in classroom learning and their academic achievement as students in the United States. These studies provide a meaningful understanding of the phenomenon of the study. Also, in this chapter, the researcher provides more details of Berry's (1997) acculturation theoretical framework, which is appropriate for exploring the phenomenon of this study.

Several researchers explored ELLs' lived experiences. The researchers found that ELLs often face acculturation experiences to integrate into the new cultural classroom learning environment (Al-Krenawi et al., 2021; Bowers et al., 2022; Hieu, 2023). The acculturation experiences faced by ELLs included English language barriers and limited cultural ability to socialize in the classroom environment (Bennouna et al., 2021; Hieu, 2023; Meng, 2020). The acculturation experiences of ELLs within the classroom in the United States have resulted in negative academic outcomes for the population of ELLs (Boileau et al., 2022). Also, ELLs often lack English language proficiency, which makes it more difficult for them to effectively succeed in the core subject areas and culturally integrate into their classroom learning environment (Bennouna et al., 2021; Hieu, 2023; Parker et al., 2021; Stark et al., 2021).

Murphy and Torff (2019) explored the experiences of ELLs. The researchers found that, academically, ELLs performed poorly compared to non-ELL students (Murphy & Torff, 2019). Also, the researchers indicated that ELLs lack English language proficiency to pass the state exams, lack motivation, and represent the lower graduation group of students (Hong et al., 2019; Shahbazi, 2020; Soland & Sandilos, 2021). Due to these challenges, ELLs face short-term and long-term educational disadvantages as students in the United States (Delgado et al., 2022; Owens & Wells, 2021; Soland & Sandilos, 2021). Therefore, Berry's (1997) acculturation theory is the fundamental and comprehensive theoretical framework that provides a meaningful understanding of the acculturation experiences of ELLs within the classroom learning environment in the United States.

This literature review includes several themes. The themes of this literature review are English language learners (ELLs), the barriers and challenges encountered by ELLs, language acquisition experiences of ELLs, ELLs' testing accommodations experiences, ELLs academic achievement experiences, ELLs' graduation rates experiences, ELLs acculturation experiences, ELLs classroom assimilation and integration experiences, ELLs self-motivation experiences and teachers of ELLs. The themes provide an in-depth understanding of the current research studies related to ELLs' acculturation, psychological, cultural, and academic lived experiences of ELLs within the classroom learning environment in the United States.

Several databases were used to access the key terms for the literature review for this study. These databases included EBSCO Host, ProQuest, Eric, and Education Search Complete. A Google Scholar search was also used to find appropriate journal articles for this literature review. Roadrunner of National University's (NU) library was used as the search engine to access relevant literature review regarding the phenomenon of this study. The theoretical framework included journal articles from the past five years to explain the framework's usefulness in the last years. The parameters for research key terms and peer review journal articles were limited from (2017-2023). Therefore, the key terms were used to find the relevant journal articles regarding the acculturation experiences and the academic achievement of the population of ELLs within the classroom learning environment in the United States: *ELLs acculturation experiences, classroom, learning environment of ELLs, English language learners (ELLs), ELLs, challenges, obstacles of ELLs, population, English language acquisition, English language, ESOL teachers, English language barriers, graduation rates, ELLs motivation, ELLs performance, ELLs academic achievement, language proficiency, teachers' perceptions of ELLs, Limited English Proficiency (LEP), teachers' beliefs, policies regarding ELLs, instructional practices of ELLs,* and *testing accommodations for ELLs.* Also, words *and* as well *or* were used to advance the search.

## Theoretical Framework

Acculturation theories have been used to explain the cultural changes immigrants face during their acculturation adventures. Some of the contributors to acculturation theories include Gordon (1964), Redfield et al. (1936), and Schumann (1978). Redfield et al. (1936) suggested that acculturation is a cultural change resulting from contact with two cultural groups. Redfield et al. (1936) noted that culture change and assimilation are part of the acculturation process. Gordon (1964) also noted that immigrants and their children acculturated, assimilated into American culture, and formed cultural pluralism. Schumann (1978) focused on the socio-psychological aspect of acculturation resulting from contact between dominant and non-dominant groups. Schumann (1978) suggested three strategies of acculturation: assimilation, preservation, and adaptation.

Therefore, Berry's (1997) acculturation theory is based on the classical definition of acculturation. According to Berry (1997), acculturation is a change between the primary and host cultures' experiences. As a result, the theoretical framework for this qualitative, descriptive phenomenological study was Berry's (1997) acculturation theory. Berry's (1997) acculturation theory focuses on the lived experiences of immigrants and their acculturation experiences with the host culture. According to Berry's (1997) acculturation theory, the host culture often influences and assimilates individuals. Berry's (1997) acculturation theory was developed to understand the process of cultural change between dominant group culture and non-dominant group culture. Berry's (1997) acculturation model has explored the psychological and behavioral changes of immigrants in Canada and presented a comprehensive picture regarding immigrant interaction within a new cultural environment. For instance, acculturation theory provides a comprehensive theoretical framework to interpret the process of cultural contact between the host group culture and the immigrant culture (Te Lindert et al., 2022).

Berry (1997) examined cross-cultural psychology and the meaning of acculturation. Berry (1997) indicated that the heritage culture can be integrated into the larger society. Berry (1997) noted that acculturation includes several components of immigrants' experiences, such as years, age, discrimination, economic status, immigration class, and social capital. According to Berry (1997), multiculturalism, cultural communities, cultural maintenance, and the need to integrate minority group cultures into a larger society are essential to acculturation. For instance, Berry's (1997) acculturation theory examines the relationship between the host and primary cultures when the immigrants attempt to establish themselves in a new country. Also, the acculturation model was used to investigate the cultural changes of immigrants and refugees in adaptation to North American, Australian, European, Asian, African, and South American cultures and settings (Berry, 1997; Guo et al., 2020).

Berry's (1997) acculturation theory includes four strategies to explain the acculturation process of immigrants. Berry's (1997) acculturation strategies are assimilation, separation, integration, and marginalization. According to Berry (1997), assimilation is the context in which individuals adopt a positive attitude toward the new culture. Also, assimilation occurs when the immigrants receive favorably the host culture and discard their heritage culture (Berry, 1997; Nguyen & Rule, 2020). For instance, in Berry's (1997) model, the assimilation strategy helps immigrants adapt to the larger society and the host culture.

Berry (1997) noted that separation is the strategy that indicates individuals maintain a positive attitude toward the primary culture. Berry (1997) stated that immigrants adapting to the separation strategy often oppose the host culture and keep their place. For example, the immigrants included in the separation strategy are usually afraid to explore the new culture and prefer to stay in their own society (Zeng et al., 2020). Also, the immigrants in the separation category lack interest in the host culture and the values of the larger society (Berry, 1997; Ugurel Kamisli, 2021).

Integration occurs when the immigrants maintain a positive attitude toward the host or the new culture and their primary culture (Berry, 1997; Kumi-Yeboah et al., 2020). For instance, immigrants tend to benefit more by selecting and utilizing the integration strategy (Berry, 1997; Zeng et al., 2020). For instance, immigrants who are influenced by the integration strategy maintain and value their primary cultural integrity while they become an integral part of the new culture society (Berry, 1997; Zeng et al., 2020). The acculturation theory notes that the integration process takes time, and individuals deal with the integration process differently (Berry, 1990).

The marginalization strategy occurs when the immigrants develop a negative attitude toward the new culture and their primary culture. Also, the marginalization strategy leads to unhealthy attitudes that are associated with poor psychological experiences (Berry, 1997). According to Berry (1997), immigrants who adopt the separation or the marginalization strategies often resist and reject the host culture. Therefore, marginalization and separation strategies have the most negative experiences and consequences on the immigrants' effort to join the new cultural environment (Berry, 1997).

In addition, Berry's (1997) acculturation theory has been used to explore immigrants' lived experiences in adapting to new cultural settings. Acculturation theory has been used to explore immigrants' transition to the host country (Berry, 1997). For instance, Berry (1997) examined immigrants' acculturation experiences by using acculturation theory. Berry and Hou (2016) used acculturation theory to explore the sense of belonging of immigrants during their transition into the new society and culture changes. The sense of belonging occurs when the immigrants feel accepted and adapted to the host country (Berry & Hou, 2016). Berry and Hou (2016) showed that the integration strategy was the most preferred strategy among Berry's acculturation strategies. Also, the results of the study indicated that social factors influenced immigrants that were associated with assimilation, separation, and marginalization strategies (Berry & Hou, 2016). However, Berry and Hou (2016) revealed that immigrants who remained in their heritage culture and engaged within the host culture achieved a greater sense of well-being.

Several existing research studies used Berry's (1997) acculturation theory. Researchers used Berry's (1997) acculturation model to investigate several aspects that shape the lived experiences and acculturation experiences of immigrants and ELLs. Liu et al. (2022) used Berry's (1997) acculturation theory to investigate Chinese international students. The total number of participants in the study was 167 Chinese international students (Liu et al., 2022). The findings of the study have revealed that acculturation stress was significant for Chinese students with mindfulness and identified that students with lower mindfulness may have a higher risk for depression and anxiety and experience more acculturation stress (Liu et al., 2022). The study's results supported Berry's acculturation model because the researchers found that the acculturation stress of the students included social isolation, academic pressure, and language insufficiency (Liu et al., 2022). The acculturative stress and psychological outcomes among Chinese international students in the United States were significant due to their experiences (Liu et al., 2022). The limitations of this study were self-reported surveys, Chinese international students, the setting of the study, and group differences among Chinese international students (Liu et al., 2022).

However, researchers suggested that other studies can compare Chinese international students with other students from different cultures (Liu et al., 2022). Similarly, Choy et al. (2021) also used acculturation theory to explore immigrants' acculturation experiences. Researchers revealed that acculturation strategies significantly impact the immigrant population (Choy et al., 2021). Like Choy et al.'s (2021) study, Pendakur (2021) used the acculturation theory to investigate immigrant children's settlement and lived experiences. The findings of this study supported the acculturation strategies (Pendakur, 2021).

Montgomery et al. (2021) utilized Berry's (1997) acculturation model theory to explore Latino immigrants' acculturation experiences in the United States. The total participants of the study were 576 Latino immigrants (Montgomery et al., 2021). Researchers revealed that the acculturation experiences challenged many immigrants (Montgomery et al., 2021). Montgomery et al. (2021) indicated that the integration strategy was the most applicable acculturation strategy that supports immigrants' lived experiences. The findings of the study highlighted that there is a need for more linguistically equitable interactions between immigrants who are ELLs and the non-ELL population (Montgomery et al., 2021). The study focused on Latino immigrants' willingness to communicate interculturally (Montgomery et al., 2021). Researchers suggested that other studies can investigate other immigrant communities (Montgomery et al., 2021). Therefore, studies by Liu et al. (2022) and Montgomery et al. (2021) supported Berry's (1997) acculturation model theory. The findings of the studies revealed that acculturation strategies were significant and applicable acculturation strategies to explore immigrants' acculturation lived experiences in the United States (Choy et al., 2021; Liu et al., 2022; Montgomery et al., 2021).

Zakarneh (2021) utilized Berry's (1997) acculturation model theory to explore sociocultural learning environments, collaboration, culture changes, and interactions with other individuals in the context of promoting assimilation, integration, and acquisition of a new language. Also, Hanfstingl et al. (2021) used the acculturation model theory to investigate the population of immigrants and their experiences. Studies noted that successful assimilation and integration contribute to more excellent academic outcomes for the immigrant population (Hanfstingl et al., 2021). Similarly, Dang et al. (2022) found that successful assimilation and integration experiences help ELLs expand their learning ability and classroom interactions, overcome their acculturation challenges, and increase their classroom cultural experiences. Mardian and Nafissi (2022) also noted that Berry's acculturation framework offers the foundational guidelines to address the acculturation experiences of ELLs by creating a cultural classroom environment that embraces diverse experiences.

The other alternative theoretical frameworks that can be used to explore the phenomenon of this study include motivation and self-determination theories. Motivation theory involves both intrinsic and extrinsic concepts (Irvine, 2018). The role of teachers is to provide a learning environment and opportunities to motivate their students (Agarkar, 2019). Motivation is why people behave in a certain manner to achieve their goals, which manifests emotionally, cognitively, and academically (Gagné & Deci, 2005; Irvine, 2018). For instance, individuals are more likely to be motivated to learn a new language that is associated with their interests and values (Irvine, 2018). Researchers stated that motivation theory is one of the frameworks in which second language acquisition can be conceptualized because learners often become more motivated if their cultural and intellectual values are found to be associated with the new language (Cho et al., 2019; Dessie & Sewagegn, 2019). Also, second language learners must demonstrate a willingness to communicate and interact with native speakers and others in the new language (Olifant et al., 2019).

The self-determination theory is another theoretical framework associated with second language acquisition (Gagné & Deci, 2005; Irvine, 2018). Researchers claim that self-determination is learners' natural curiosity for flourishing and academic achievement (Goldman et al., 2018). For instance, researchers indicated that the self-determination theory framework is applicable when individuals have positive perceptions about themselves (Dessie & Sewagegn, 2019; Olifant et al., 2019). Also, self-confidence and self-determination are essential aspects of learning the English language as a second language because intrinsically motivated ELLs tend to find more pleasure in learning and, as a result, become more successful as students (Irvine, 2018). Therefore, motivation and self-determination frameworks offer a less comprehensive framework that can be used to explore ELLs' acculturation experiences and cultural differences (Gagné & Deci, 2005; Irvine, 2018). These theoretical frameworks are not suitable for describing the acculturation experiences of ELLs within the classroom learning environment. Therefore, motivation and self-determination are not considered when exploring the phenomenon of the study (Burn & Menter, 2021; Duran, 2022).

Therefore, Berry's (1997) acculturation theory was chosen to explore the lived experiences of ELLs within the classroom learning environment. Lai et al. (2023) and Olds et al. (2021) emphasized that individuals interact within the social and cultural environment contexts that influence their learning experiences. Also, Berry's (1997) acculturation theoretical framework is suitable for exploring cultural learning environments, cultural changes, individuals' interactions, and individuals' experiences in the context of promoting assimilation, integration, acquiring new perspectives, and adapting to a new culture, language, and learning environment (Montgomery et al., 2021; Zakarneh, 2021). Berry's (1997) acculturation theory includes four acculturation strategies that indicate the experiences of immigrants in the host country, and these strategies can be applied to support ELLs' classroom interactions.

According to Montgomery et al. (2021) and Lee et al. (2023), cultural classroom learning strategies are the most significant factors in helping ELLs overcome their challenges and increase their classroom integration development process. Therefore, Berry's (1997) acculturation framework provides the critical implications and strategies to promote a successful acculturation experience, improve the learning experience, and increase the academic achievement of ELLs. For instance, these strategies provide extensive knowledge to create a cultural classroom learning environment that embraces the diverse experiences of ELLs (Burn & Menter, 2021; Duran, 2022).

Berry's (1997) acculturation theory was also used to explore the acculturation experiences of ELLs because the separation and marginalization strategies often contribute to poor academic achievement. On the other hand, the assimilation and integration strategies contribute to greater academic outcomes for the population of immigrants (Berry, 1997; Burn & Menter, 2021; Duran, 2022). The acculturation theory provides evidence-based strategies to understand the immigrants' cultural changes, language barrier experiences, attitudes, and behaviors toward the new cultural learning environment (Berry, 2015; Burn & Menter, 2021; Duran, 2022). Researchers noted that assimilation and integration are essential to help ELLs expand their learning abilities, overcome their acculturation challenges, and increase their classroom integration experiences (Dang et al., 2022; Sousa et al., 2019). This theoretical framework offers the foundational guidelines to address the acculturation experiences of ELLs by creating a cultural classroom environment that embraces diverse experiences (Mardian & Nafissi, 2022; Olds et al., 2021). Also, this framework provides the most effective strategies that include teaching practices, cultural engagement, home language encouragement, cultural instructional practices that facilitate learning, collaborative classroom discussions regarding cultural diversity, and improved acculturation experiences of the ELLs (Dang et al., 2022).

Berry's (1997) acculturation theory was aligned with the purpose, the problem statement, and the research questions of the study. Using Berry's (1997) acculturation theory, this study may help teachers and others realize that learning the English language is a process that includes the

ELLs' experiences. It may help teachers understand that ELLs are coming from different perspectives, and these perspectives include ELLs' own cultural backgrounds and the learning styles they bring into their classroom environment as learners (Antoniadou & Quinlan, 2020; Choy et al., 2021). Acculturation theory maintains that linguistic environment, cultural values, and beliefs are essential for individuals to develop effective language skills in the host country (Berry, 1997). Therefore, Berry's (1997) acculturation theory provides the most effective strategies that include teaching practices, cultural engagement, home language encouragement, cultural and instructional practices that facilitate learning, collaborative classroom discussions regarding cultural diversity, and enhancing the acculturation experiences of the ELLs. Therefore, by using Berry's (1997) acculturation theory, this study addressed ELLs' acculturation experiences and lower academic achievement experiences.

## English Language Learners (ELLs)

ELLs are students whose primary language is not English; they speak another language at home yet seek education in United States schools (Balilah & Archibald, 2022; Kennedy & McLoughlin, 2023; Meng, 2020). Andrei and Northrop (2022) found that ELLs constitute the most critical group of students in the United States public schools, and approximately 10% of K-12 students are ELLs across the nation's schools. The studies revealed that the population of ELLs has increased over the years in all schools in the United States, and ELLs are also considered one of the fastest-growing groups of students across public schools (Lowenhaupt et al., 2020; Meng, 2020; Song, 2022; Watkinson et al., 2022). The increase in the ELL population is an alarming issue for many educators and states due to their limited English proficiency (LEP) and the challenges of meeting their academic needs (Kennedy & McLoughlin, 2023). For instance, Kennedy and McLoughlin (2023) claimed that one in five students in the United States are ELLs because their primary language is not English; they face significant challenges, and their needs are unique due to their cultural and language differences. Indeed, ELLs differ from native English-speaking students in several ways: they must learn grade-level content while acquiring English language skills (Balilah & Archibald, 2022). Also, ELLs tend to struggle with all kinds of English language skills, such as reading, writing, listening, and speaking skills (Kennedy & McLoughlin, 2023).

According to De Valenzuela et al. (2022), one of the procedures for identifying ELLs is to have a home language survey completed by their parents or guardians. In addition, if the parent acknowledges that the primary home language is another language other than English language and positively answers any of the following three questions:

1. What is the primary language used at home by the student?
2. 2What language is most used by the student?
3. What is the language that the student first acquired?

De Valenzuela et al. (2022) noted that if a parent responds in the language survey with a language other than English, then the student needs to undergo tests for English proficiency. On the other hand, if the parent states that English is the primary language used at home, the given school does not need to test the student in terms of language proficiency (De Valenzuela et al., 2022). Similarly, Lowenhaupt et al. (2020) emphasized the importance of accurately determining who qualifies as an ELL. Lowenhaupt et al. (2020) claimed that it is important to determine who can be termed as ELLs and appropriately allocate the placement of ELLs to measure their English language proficiency. Lowenhaupt et al. (2020) indicated that a test is administered to all ELLs, from kindergarten to the twelfth grade, whose primary language is not English language. Lowenhaupt et al.'s (2020) research further supported the significance of the procedures outlined by de Valenzuela et al. (2022).

Kennedy and McLoughlin (2023) conducted a quantitative study to explore the literacy skills of ELLs. Researchers claimed that one of the significant concerns about ELLs is that teachers who work with ELLs think that some of the ELLs lack background knowledge about their first language, which impacts their ability to ensure progress in all five key English language components: listening, speaking, reading, writing, and included vocabulary (Kennedy & McLoughlin, 2023; Maarouf, 2019). However, a second language refers to the language spoken by an individual who already has a native language (Kennedy & McLoughlin, 2023). Kennedy and McLoughlin (2023) revealed that there is a relationship between students' skills in their native language and their achievement concerning the second language. Researchers indicated that ELLs performed lower in terms of English Language Arts (ELA) and math (Kennedy & McLoughlin, 2023). The findings of the quantitative study revealed that English language skills are essential for developing a successful learning experience for ELLs (Kennedy & McLoughlin, 2023).

Also, Arellano et al. (2018) explored ELLs learning experiences. Researchers noted that many students identified as ELLs in kindergarten also required at least three to four years of instruction after kindergarten to reach an optimal level of English proficiency (Arellano et al., 2018; Khoo & Kang, 2022). For instance, researchers claimed that many students had not been considered proficient in English before leaving elementary schools, and only a small percentage of ELLs who were reclassified as fluent in English demonstrated readiness concerning English Language Arts (ELA) and mathematics (Arellano et al., 2018). The study's findings revealed that many ELLs did not reach grade-level readiness in terms of ELA and mathematics before they exited the ESOL programs (Arellano et al., 2018). Maarouf (2019) explored the academic growth of ELLs. ELLs face similar challenges in meeting academic levels in the reading curriculum (Maarouf, 2019).

## The Barriers and Challenges Encountered by ELLs

The barriers experienced by ELLs have significantly impacted the acculturation and academic achievement experiences of ELLs (Dewi et al., 2021). Dewi et al. (2021) explored the English language and cultural barriers of ELLs. Researchers claimed that English language barriers are part of the challenges faced by ELLs and immigrant students (Dewi et al., 2021; Hsin et al., 2022). According to Dewi et al. (2021), the English language barriers ELLs face include communication, sociocultural interactions, limited English language skills, and a lack of ability to express their ideas. The findings of Dewi et al.'s (2021) study revealed that English language barriers impacted ELLs' ability to make friends with native language speakers, understand work materials, and engage in their classroom interactions and activities. Similarly, Casey et al. (2020) explored the effectiveness of English and Spanish picture books to support ELLs. Researchers also claimed that ELLs face countless challenges in core science, mathematics, and social studies classes due to English language barriers (Casey et al., 2020).

In addition, Lee and Orgill (2022) explored equitable assessments related to ELLs. Researchers claimed that ELLs face basic English vocabulary, content vocabulary, and language structures (Lee & Orgill, 2022). The findings of Lee and Orgill's (2022) study revealed that English language barriers are one of the main challenges that impact ELLs' academic performance. Also, the findings of Casey et al.'s (2020) and Dewi et al.'s (2021) studies indicated that ELLs face language barriers in passing the core English language assessments.

Dursun and Sevim (2022) investigated the challenges encountered by foreign students. Researchers found that English language skills are critical for culture adaptation, integration, academic achievement, and school interactions (Dursun & Sevim, 2022). Researchers noted that the English language barriers also affected ELLs' confidence in their English language abilities to share their cultural experiences and opinions (Dursun & Sevim, 2022). According to Horne (2021), English language barriers become a challenge for ELLs to demonstrate their cultural knowledge and academic competency. The English language barriers also contribute to ELLs' low academic performance and high dropout rates compared to non-ELL students (Horne, 2021).

The barriers faced by ELLs are often associated with behavior issues such as the academic learning environment, limited education, lack of knowledge, limited support, and discrimination (Dursun & Sevim, 2022). The findings of the study revealed that language barriers make learning more difficult for ELLs to acclimate to their learning environment and adapt to classroom culture, their teachers, and their classmates (Dursun & Sevim, 2022; Hsin et al., 2022). Researchers claimed that students who lack English language proficiency also face acculturative stress, depression, helplessness, and anxiety (Dursun & Sevim, 2022). Also, Hawkins et al. (2022) revealed that acculturation is the process by which individuals change their values and their primary language as they are assimilated into another culture. Hawkins et al. (2022) found that English language proficiency and the new cultural environment are barriers that create a huge challenge for ELLs. For example, researchers noted that ELLs face social and cultural challenges that contribute to more stressful learning experiences (Hawkins et al., 2022). The ELLs who face English language proficiency also face additional barriers to adapting to the new learning environment (Lewis & Brown, 2021). The additional barriers faced by ELLs include difficulty participating in their classroom discussions and sharing their own experiences with classmates (Lewis & Brown, 2021). Researchers revealed that engaging and supporting ELLs to achieve academic and cultural success are essential factors in helping

ELLs overcome their language barriers and acculturation experiences (Lewis & Brown, 2021).

Lim et al. (2021) explored Spanish-speaking immigrant parents. The study found that 40% of ELLs in the U.S. face limited English proficiency. Researchers claimed that the language barriers, including a lack of skills and abilities in the English language to communicate with others, contributed to the poor experiences and outcomes of the ELLs (Lim et al., 2021). The study revealed that ELLs need verbal communication skills in order to share their experiences because ELLs who do not have English language skills tend to separate themselves from the host culture (Lim et al., 2021). Also, Hussain et al. (2020) indicated that English language and communication barriers are not related only to acculturation experiences but also represent a disadvantage for the population of ELLs. For instance, the English language barrier is related to many experiences faced by ELLs in their classroom learning environment (Guler, 2020).

Garcia et al. (2019) examined ELLs English language proficiency. Researchers found that limited language English proficiency contributed to the poor academic outcomes of ELLs (Garcia et al., 2019). According to Garcia et al. (2019), many teachers do not demonstrate persistence with respect to improving the academic outcomes of their ELLs as students. For instance, many teachers underrate the academic skills of many ELLs compared to their native English-speaking students (Stairs-Davenport, 2023). Also, Huang (2022) claimed that limited English proficiency means less access for ELLs. The researcher also noted that teachers might have more long-term impacts on ELLs 'academic achievements (Huang, 2022). However, many teachers do not understand the gravity and challenges faced by their ELLs (Huang, 2022). For example, teachers may have a greater impact on their students who struggle with English proficiency (Huang, 2022). In addition, ELLs are regarded by their teachers as incompetent and lazy when they face academic difficulties due to the notion that their parents are irresponsible and contributed to their failures (Garcia et al., 2019). ELLs do not fully benefit from the great educational system, and they do not receive a fair education (Garcia et al., 2019). According to Yamauchi et al. (2022), the needs of ELLs are unique and require appropriate prescriptions regardless of their backgrounds. Yamauchi et al. (2022) noted that teachers must understand the challenges and why ELLs face difficulties in reaching English proficiency levels and academic success. However, researchers found a lack of understanding regarding how teachers describe ELLs' challenges (Protacio et al., 2020). Protacio et al. (2020) noted that teachers need to become more proactive in the approaches and strategies they use to meet the needs of their ELLs. The findings of the study have revealed that ELLs 'academic achievements are not equal to the academic achievement of native English-speaking students (Protacio et al., 2020).

Lee et al. (2020) explored ELLs in the science classrooms. Lee et al. (2020) indicated that ELLs had not experienced poor acculturation across all school settings in the United States only but lacked intrinsic motivation to achieve cognitive academic language proficiency. The researchers claimed that ELLs need cognitive academic language proficiency to pass standardized assessments as well as to remain more successful throughout their academic years (Lee et al., 2020). Also, Stairs-Davenport (2023) stated that academic language proficiency is related to teachers' and ELLs' interactions. ELLs benefit more when teachers allow and encourage their students to display their understanding of certain content via multiple venues (Stairs-Davenport, 2023). Furthermore, ELLs learn more from their interactions in the language to be learned when they can express themselves instead of getting intimidated by the English language and its native speakers (Stairs-Davenport, 2023). Hussain et al. (2020) stated that ELLs lacked extrinsic and intrinsic motivation due to English language proficiency. Researchers claimed that the lack of motivation also impacted the ability of ELLs in reading, science, and math academic achievement. The findings of this study revealed that ELLs faced unfavorable positions to succeed compared to English-speaking students (Björling et al., 2021; Gupta, 2019; Hussain et al., 2020).

Shahbazi (2020) explored the lived experiences of teachers and their perceptions towards the integration of ELLs. The study indicated that ELLs face challenges that include English language instruction resources that are academically, socially, and culturally appropriate to their experiences and interests (Shahbazi, 2020). The study has found that teaching ELLs requires several approaches teachers can use to assist their students (Shahbazi, 2020). The most important and successful approach to learning the English language is to encourage ELLs to read books suited to their proficiency levels (Shahbazi, 2020). Moreover, Artigliere (2019) explored the proficiency, instructional, and effective methods of long-term support for ELLs. The researcher claimed that the most effective method to help ELLs is to encourage them to read books in their own language, promote appropriate levels of reading achievement in English, and promote bilingual skills (Artigliere, 2019). The study noted that language plays critical roles, which are not only limited to transmitting information but also equip ELLs with the means to assimilate and adapt to the new cultural environment (Artigliere, 2019). The findings of the study revealed that experienced teachers assist their ELLs in overcoming their English language challenges and barriers (Artigliere, 2019).

Similarly, Min et al. (2023) explored elementary teachers' beliefs on culturally and linguistically teaching ELLs. Researchers noted that the increasing number of ELLs in public schools in the United States and also their academic performance is lower than that of their peers (Min et al., 2023). Researchers revealed that, culturally and linguistically, students are underrepresented, and classroom teachers can implement pedagogies that could support all students (Min et al., 2023). According to Min et al. (2023), ELLs need academic vocabulary, academic literacy, academic language, and a learning environment that connects their lived experiences and their existing skills. Therefore, a favorable cultural learning environment and culturally appropriate pedagogy are essential in supporting ELLs' classroom learning experiences (Roman & Nunez, 2020; Shahbazi, 2020).

In addition, Madler et al. (2022) explored teachers' perceptions toward classroom diversity population students. Researchers claimed that teachers need to provide effective instruction, a learning environment and cultural competence, that are important for a diverse classroom environment (Madler et al., 2022). Researchers indicated that the diversity among learners includes language, cultural background, learning approaches, and academic needs that demand instructional and cultural strategies to ensure positive learning experiences for ELLs (Madler et al., 2022). The findings of the studies revealed that the perceptions of teachers to provide cultural instruction to support ELLs' acculturation lived experiences declined because a great number of teachers perceived that they are underprepared to meet the needs of a diverse population of ELLs (Gupta, 2019; Madler et al., 2022).

Kapoyannis (2021) investigated teachers who have experience working with ELLs. According to Kapoyannis (2021), the population of students is increasingly becoming more linguistically and culturally diverse due to the current influx of ELLs. Kapoyannis (2021) noted that ELLs are often in the classrooms that have less qualified teachers (Kapoyannis, 2021). Therefore, the wide achievement gaps between ELLs and native English speakers show the need to have more qualified teachers to teach ELLs (Kapoyannis, 2021). Kapoyannis (2021) noted ELLs face difficulties fitting in and tend to feel like outsiders in their own schools and that it is the teachers' duty to provide classroom environments that support ELLs' academic achievement. The findings of the study revealed that a cultural and safe learning environment are essential strategies to support ELLs in assimilating into their classroom settings (Kapoyannis, 2021). For instance, Murray (2020) explored ELLs adjustment anxieties. The population of ELLs includes diverse backgrounds (Murray, 2020). The culturally diversified groups of ELLs often faced challenges and experienced limited English language proficiency (Ben et al., 2023; Murray, 2020). As a result, ELLs have a tremendous deficiency in academic language, which can serve as a barrier in many areas (Murray, 2020).

Also, Watkinson et al. (2022) explored school counselors who worked with ELLs. Researchers claim that ELLs are one of the increasing student groups in the U.S., but school counselors are unprepared to address the challenges faced by ELLs (Watkinson et al., 2022). According to Watkinson et al. (2022), the challenges faced by ELLs include learning the English language, academic gaps, school adaptation, and assimilation to the new school environment. The findings of the study revealed that the need to address the challenges faced by ELLs includes academic support, classroom integration, and acculturation support because ELLs are isolated and experience disadvantages in their new classroom learning environment (Watkinson et al., 2022).

Davis and Tesh (2022) explored ELLs' learning experiences. Researchers claimed that the change in environment made it difficult for the population of ELLs in the United States (Davis & Tesh, 2022). The challenges experienced by many ELLs include a lack of technology skills, limited comprehension of English language skills, social isolation, and poor motivation (Davis & Tesh, 2022). According to Yoon (2021), ELLs have more stressful experiences due to the pressure from perceptions and expectations to achieve academic success. Also, ELLs tend to demonstrate that their adaptation experiences and academic achievement have not changed significantly (Yoon, 2021). For instance, De Araujo and Smith (2022) stated that ELLs felt that they did not belong in their classrooms because they were treated poorly and shamed, along with being perceived as the lower group of students. Indeed, ELLs are more likely to suffer from poor academic performance (De Araujo & Smith, 2022). The researchers claimed that when ELLs discover that little is expected from them, they may respond negatively by performing at the expected lower levels because many teachers have different perceptions of ELLs compared to native students (Davis &Tesh, 2022). ELLs have difficulties adhering to the existing teaching and learning methods, and they are perceived as inferior and suffer from stereotyping and discriminatory practices (Murray, 2020). ELLs also receive less academic support from their teachers and lack resources, perceptions, cultural differences, and the ability to teach all kinds of students effectively (Murray, 2020).

## Language Acquisition Experiences of ELLs

Acquiring another language is a challenge that is influenced by several factors, such as the individual's native language background, learning environment experience, and the nuances of English language grammar and pronunciation (Saito et al., 2018). These factors create a unique challenge for ELLs (Saito et al., 2018; Wei, 2021). Also, researchers claimed that the challenges faced by ELLs are related to linguistic, emotional, and cultural elements that impact their learning experiences (Gupta,

2019; Maarouf, 2019; Saito et al., 2018; Wei, 2021). Saito et al. (2018) explored the differences between ELLs' primary language skills and their ability to learn the English language. Researchers claimed that children learn their first language naturally from their familial environments and their school settings (Saito et al., 2018). The researchers noted that the first language of the learners influences their quality of learning and utilization of their second language (Saito et al., 2018; Wei, 2021). Also, researchers further asserted that with respect to English as a second language, there is a difference between mastering the rules of grammar and spoken English pronunciation (Saito et al., 2018). Mastery of English grammatical rules does not automatically ensure the correct functional use of the English language (Saito et al., 2018; Song, 2022). The first language may have a syllable structure that is different from the English language (Saito et al., 2018). According to Saito et al. (2018), there is a difference in learning pronunciations, formation, and rules that compose the English language. Similarly, Wei (2021) explored ELLs and stated that ELLs in K-12 grades are struggling to become fluent in English. Also, Gupta (2019) stated that cultural context is the first step in building effective literacy programs that are inclusive to meet the needs of ELLs. However, the findings of the study revealed that motivated ELLs can finally master the grammatical rules and acquire English language skills (Gupta, 2019; Saito et al., 2018).

Schneider and Kulmhofer-Bommer (2022) investigated the second language acquisition process among ELLs. The researchers claimed that the second language acquisition process is based on the accommodation hypothesis (Schneider & Kulmhofer-Bommer, 2022). The authors pointed out that individuals, in general, have an extremely unique ability to learn several languages (Schneider & Kulmhofer-Bommer, 2022). In addition, Hartshorne et al. (2018) explored the second language acquisition experiences of ELLs. Researchers claimed that people who learn a second language at an early age develop accents that are similar to the native speakers of the language (Hartshorne et al., 2018). Also, Hartshorne et al. (2018) noted that people who begin to learn a second language upon attaining adulthood often tend to have accent-related and grammatical difficulties. The differences between children and adults learning a second language are due to the plasticity of the brain and the role of neural maturation in learning (Hartshorne et al., 2018; LaScotte, 2020; Sinha, 2021). The findings of the study revealed that ELLs can achieve English language proficiency if only they persist long enough to deploy their conscious strategies and transfer their first-language knowledge to understand and grasp the new language (Hartshorne et al., 2018).

## ELLs Testing Accommodations Experiences

ELLs also face acculturation experiences related to classroom testing accommodations (Abedi et al., 2020). The testing accommodations are provided to all ELLs to help them overcome the English language barriers, academic achievement, and classroom acculturation experiences (Abedi et al., 2020). Abedi et al. (2020) examined the effectiveness and validity of accommodations used to support the learning experiences of ELLs. Policies across the United States have affected ELLs' learning experiences (Abedi et al., 2020). The policies not only deny ELLs their native language and culture effective support, but these policies also set up ELLs for academic failure (Abedi et al., 2020). For example, Yough et al. (2023) noted that graduation rates of ELLs are considerably lower compared to those of their peers, which may have negative implications for educational opportunities for ELLs.

The researchers indicated that the elimination of bilingual education contributed to the low performance of non-English-speaking students who are ELLs (Abedi et al., 2020). Also, researchers noted that policies that embrace language diversity, preparation, and pedagogical skills make a more positive difference in learning experiences (Abedi et al., 2020). Nerlinger (2021) explored testing accommodations that are provided to ELLs. The study noted that teachers must provide testing accommodations to assist their ELLs and allow them to demonstrate their proficiency on these standardized assessments (Nerlinger, 2021). However, testing accommodations do not intend to provide advantages to ELLs over English-speaking students (Nerlinger, 2021). Instead, testing accommodations are provided to help ELLs meet their own challenges (Nerlinger, 2021). According to Buono and Jang (2021), testing accommodations address the English language issues and some specific skills that make the English language a less major factor when measuring the performance of ELLs. The researchers revealed that testing accommodations are critical for ELLs' academic achievement, specifically to ameliorate their English language barriers (Buono & Jang, 2021). The most common accommodations for ELLs include extended time to complete tests, flexible settings, heritage dictionaries, and glossaries with translations of non-content words (Buono & Jang, 2021; Nerlinger, 2021). The findings of the study revealed that effective accommodations may help ELLs perform and achieve greater academic scores in the core content areas (Nerlinger, 2021).

## ELLs' Academic Achievement Experiences

The acculturation experiences faced by ELLs within their classroom have multiple implications (Owens & Wells, 2021). For instance, acculturative stress has significantly impacted ELLs' abilities, contributed to more English language deficiency and language barriers, and resulted in negative academic consequences (Gilblom et al., 2022; Ma & Xia, 2021). Such implications create an important academic challenge for the population of ELLs (Owens & Wells, 2021). ELLs' academic achievement is significantly lower than that of non-ELL students (Owens & Wells, 2021). Owens and Wells (2021) explored elementary teachers' perceptions regarding ELLs' academic achievement experiences. The data for this qualitative descriptive study were collected from nine elementary school teachers (Owens & Wells, 2021). Researchers noted a clear pattern of performance gaps between ELLs and English-speaking students (Owens & Wells, 2021). The achievement gap between ELLs and native students remains a serious challenge (Garcia-Borrego et al., 2020; Huang, 2022; Owens & Wells, 2021).

The performance scores of ELLs are significantly lower than those of non-ELLs in reading and math in elementary school, especially among ELLs in public schools (Maarouf, 2019). Also, researchers noted that scholars, school district personnel, and lawmakers are searching for the best teaching strategies that would enable teachers to meet the needs of

ELLs, including English proficiency and a cultural classroom learning environment (Guler, 2020; Owens & Wells, 2021). Researchers indicated that ELLs feel more comfortable when their teachers provide cultural stories and opportunities to integrate their prior knowledge, which includes native language literacy skills (Owens & Wells, 2021). However, the study indicated that ELLs are more comfortable taking risks when they feel safe, supported, and celebrated by their teachers (Maarouf, 2019). Furthermore, teachers tend to have a greater impact on their students when they create, promote, and support the cultural uniqueness and academic achievements of all students (Lewis & Brown, 2021). ELLs also feel at ease when their teachers demonstrate confidence in their abilities, regardless of their cultural and linguistic experiences (Owens & Wells, 2021). Researchers claimed that teachers are more effective when they integrate the values and prior experiences of their ELLs, pair bilingual students, provide individual assistance, and use culturally relevant stories (Owens & Wells, 2021). The findings of the study revealed that building a culturally appropriate learning environ-ment and a welcoming learning atmosphere increases the academic achievement of ELLs (Owens & Wells, 2021).

Zhang et al. (2022) examined the academic skills of ELLs. Researchers claimed that ELLs endured many challenges that included cultural, linguistic, and lower academic achievement (Zhang et al., 2022). The academic achievements of ELLs are problematic and alarming (Huang, 2022; Zhang et al., 2022). Researchers stated that the reading scores for fourth, eighth, and twelfth grades among ELLs were significantly lower compared to their peers (Zhang et al., 2022). For instance, only 1% of ELLs met the proficient level compared to 31% of non-ELLs in eighth through twelfth grades (Zhang et al., 2022). ELLs also face grammatical, syntactical, and vocabulary challenges during writing production (Zhang et al., 2022). Researchers evaluated 34 ELLs and revealed that English language skills are essential for ELLs to be successful academically, socially, and culturally (Zhang et al., 2022). Also, English language skills are vital for ELLs' literacy development, academic achievement, and cultural experiences (Huang, 2022; Zhang et al., 2022).

Similarly, Garcia-Borrego et al. (2020) explored third and fourth-grade ELLs' academic achievement. Researchers claimed that ELLs performed lower in all core subjects than regular students (Garcia-Borrego et al., 2020). The findings of the study revealed that there is a 37% gap between ELLs and their peers (Garcia-Borrego et al., 2020). The researchers noted ELLs' academic performance is a national issue because the dropout rates among ELLs are higher than their peers (Garcia-Borrego et al., 2020). The academic gaps between ELLs and non-ELL students persist due to ELLs' struggle to develop English language skills (Garcia-Borrego et al., 2020). Notably, many teachers tend to have much lower academic expectations regarding ELLs (Cho et al., 2019; Dessie & Sewagegn, 2019). The current issues of ELLs have increased the need to provide relevant education to meet the needs of the ELL population (Cho et al., 2019; Dessie & Sewagegn, 2019).

## ELLs' Graduation Rates Experiences

The acculturation experiences encountered by ELLs within their classroom learning environment have also impacted their academic achievement as students in the United States (Huck, 2021; Yough et al., 2023). Studies have found that acculturative stress has contributed to language barriers and resulted in negative academic consequences (Gilblom et al., 2022; Ma & Xia, 2021). Also, researchers indicated that acculturation experiences often lead to psychosocial issues that impact the academic performance and risk of dropping out of school and negatively shape the graduation rates of ELLs (Bennouna et al., 2021; Hieu, 2023; Murray, 2020; Soland & Sandilos, 2021). The graduation rates of ELLs represent a major concern compared to other students (Owens & Wells, 2021). According to Owens and Wells (2021), the graduation rate in the state of Virginia is about 92% among mainstream students. But the graduation rate among ELLs is 82% (Owens & Wells, 2021). Also, ELLs are behind on the state assessments (Olds et al., 2021). Similarly, researchers claimed that overall, ELLs performed below their grade level compared to their peers (Olds et al., 2021). In addition, Huck (2021) explored graduation rates and postsecondary outcomes of ELLs in Florida. The researcher noted that graduation from high school is a vital and important step for ELLs (Huck, 2021).

In addition, Yough et al. (2023) noted that graduation rates have long-term implications for ELLs' future lives, such as educational opportunities and economic independence. The study claimed that ELLs are the fastest-growing among the student population, but a great number of ELLs have experienced some challenges in achieving academic success and graduating from high school (Huck, 2021). The researcher revealed that fourth-grade ELLs' achievement scores are lower compared to non-ELL students in math; the gaps persist through high school, and that affects ELLs' graduation rates (Huck, 2021). The high school graduation rate of ELLs nationally was 68.4% in 2017–18 compared to 84% among non-ELL students (Huck, 2021). The findings of the study indicated that the school dropout risk is higher among ELLs compared to mainstream students because ELLs lacked English language skills, faced significant disadvantages, had poor learning experiences, and lacked equal opportunities (Huck, 2021). The researcher noted that ELLs are often beginning to develop their cultural English language proficiency while they are learning the core content areas. Therefore, native language assessments should be considered as a testing accommodation to support and increase the graduation rate of ELLs (Huck, 2021).

Amaro-Jiménez et al. (2020) explored culturally and linguistically diverse students.

Researchers indicated that culturally and linguistically diverse minority students are increasing from the K–12th grade population (Amaro-Jiménez et al., 2020). The high school graduation rate has increased in the U.S., but disparities continue to persist in the ELL population (Amaro-Jiménez et al., 2020). Also, according to Björling et al. (2021), the experiences of ELLs are alarming. Also, Camping et al. (2023) found that ELLs are the fastest-growing group of students in the United States public school. Researchers claimed that ELLs not only face low English proficiency challenges but also immigration and sociocultural challenges (Björling et al., 2021; Amaro-Jiménez et al., 2020). Researchers revealed that the graduation rates of ELLs are below expectations compared to their counterparts (Amaro-Jiménez et al., 2020). The findings of the study indicated that ELLs are at risk of not graduating from high school promptly because they face several significant academic challenges, and often, their schools do not create appropriate cultural learning environments to enable ELLs to mitigate and decrease their lower graduation rates experiences (Amaro-Jiménez et al., 2020).

## ELLs Acculturation Experiences

The population of ELLs in the United States faces multiple unprecedented acculturation experiences and challenges (Lomotey et al., 2020; Yingling, 2023). The acculturation experiences faced by ELLs are related to the challenges of learning the English language, socioculturally, low academic achievement, low self-motivation, and difficulties integrating into the school culture environment (Khoo & Kang, 2022; Schneider & Kulmhofer-Bommer, 2022; Watkinson et al., 2022; Wei, 2021). Stark et al. (2021) noted that ELLs often experience poor acculturation due to difficulties assimilating into new cultural classroom environments. Parker et al. (2021) defined acculturation as the acquisition of a new culture and the assimilation of the new changes. Also, Parker et al. (2021) noted that acculturation may be a challenge in building social relationships within the classroom due to a lack of English proficiency, social communication skills, social isolation, and loneliness. For instance, Stark et al. (2021) conducted similar research; they found that acculturation experiences often manifested as worry, fear, embarrassment, frustration, and anxiety in ELLs in the new classroom learning environment.

The acculturation experiences increase the stress on the ELLs, and such experiences interfere with their motivation to engage in their classroom interactions (Stark et al., 2021). The findings of the study revealed that ELLs suffered from cultural exclusion and experienced cultural disadvantages in their classroom (Stark et al., 2021). Similarly, Wang and Yu (2021) argued and advocated for socially, culturally relevant, and inclusive classrooms for ELLs in the U.S. education system. Wang and Yu (2021) claimed that a positive acculturation experience is essential for

ELLs to learn the English language effectively, and it is critical for their academic achievement.

Mastery of the English language is one of the challenges ELLs face (Wei, 2021). Also, Olifant et al. (2019) noted that mastery of the English language is vital for ELLs' success. For instance, Dessie and Sewagegn (2019) indicated that learning the English language effectively is imperative for ELLs not only for academic advancement but also to obtain more social and economic opportunities. The studies have found that ELLs need to be supported more by their teachers during second language acquisition and adaptation to the new classroom learning environment (Dessie & Sewagegn, 2019; Panunciar et al., 2022).

The current issues of ELLs have increased the need to provide a relevant cultural classroom learning environment to meet the needs of all ELLs (Dessie & Sewagegn, 2019). For instance, Dessie and Sewagegn (2019) further emphasized that teachers have a great influence on the acculturation experiences and academic achievement of ELLs by creating classroom environments that are conducive to meeting the needs of their ELLs as students. Also, researchers noted that teachers need to have appropriate and relevant cultural expectations regarding their ELLs (Dessie & Sewagegn, 2019). Several studies supported Dessie and Sewagegn's (2019) study regarding ELLs. For instance, Davis and Tesh (2022) noted that ELLs often tend to be embarrassed and refuse to participate in their classroom discussions when the classroom is not conducive to their new experiences. Also, the findings of Cho et al. (2019) and Hong et al. (2019) supported the claim that the lack of English language proficiency and the challenges of assimilating into the new school culture create the most disadvantaged and labeled ELLs as the nation's lowest academic performing group of students in the United States. Researchers argued that ELLs can learn more effectively if the classroom environment is culturally safe, relevant, and supported by the teachers (Cho et al., 2019; Hong et al., 2019).

Furthermore, the researchers highlighted that ELLs' unfavorable acculturation experiences are not without consequences (Kraus, 2023; Zhang et al., 2022). Also, Gilblom et al. (2022) noted that the poor experiences and challenges ELLs face in their classroom have learning and academic implications. For instance, Watkinson et al. (2022) claimed that there is a direct relationship between the acculturation experiences and adaptation to a new culture learning environment. Similarly, Gilblom et al.'s (2022) study revealed that poor acculturation experiences and acculturative stress have significantly impacted ELLs, contributed to more English language deficiency and language barriers, and resulted in negative academic consequences. Researchers emphasized ELLs' acculturation experiences and attitudes toward the new cultural learning environment (Gilblom et al., 2022). The findings of Gilblom et al.'s (2022) study showed that positive attitudes regarding the new culture environment increase the academic achievement of the learners, which is similar to the findings of Fang's (2020) study that indicated positive acculturation experiences are essential to greater academic achievement of ELLs. The researchers noted that cultural inclusion in the classroom environment is critical to developing a new culture, positive academic performance, and reducing the stigma of poor acculturation experiences of ELLs (Gilblom et al., 2022). The studies highlighted that unfavorable and negative acculturation experiences have contributed to more social, emotional, and behavioral challenges and lower academic achievements of the learners (Gilblom et al., 2022; Fang, 2020; Zhang et al., 2022).

ELLs' acculturation challenges include several aspects (Bennouna et al., 2021; Hieu, 2023). These aspects are related to linguistic, socioemotional, and sociocultural challenges that influence the acculturation experiences of ELLs (Bennouna et al., 2021). The researchers claimed that English language competency is one of the components of the acculturation process (Bennouna et al., 2021; Hieu, 2023; Meng, 2020). Similarly, Zaidi et al. (2021) indicated that the acculturation process includes the development of the English language, such as the language of the host culture. Researchers claimed that, generally, the English language has a direct implication in the acculturation experiences of ELLs because it helps them build their relationships with others (Bennouna et al., 2021; Hieu, 2023). In addition, Luo et al. (2021) found that one of the challenges in the process of acculturation is that ELLs are often instructed by teachers who do not share the same language and cultural backgrounds as the ELLs acculturation experiences. Luo et al.'s (2021) study revealed that appropriate English language acculturation processes and experiences help ELLs to improve their ability to communicate with other individuals, both psychologically and academically integrated into the mainstream English language and learning environment culture. The findings of Hieu's (2023) and Meng's (2020) studies noted that ELLs' attitudes and beliefs toward new cultural change and psychological change toward mainstream culture are important for their success because ELLs tend to experience difficulties such as language barrier, higher expectations, difficulty understanding lectures in English, and the challenges to integrate into the new classroom learning environment.

## ELLs Classroom Assimilation and Integration Experiences

According to Shahbazi (2020), ELLs face many challenges in assimilation and integration into their classroom learning environment. The study also indicated that acquiring a new culture and assimilating to a new learning experience often represent the biggest challenges for the population of ELLs (Shahbazi, 2020). Wang and Zhou (2021) explored the assimilation experiences of ELLs. Studies have found that ELLs arriving in the United States often face several cultural challenges and culture shock as they integrate into the new environment (Wang & Zhou, 2021). Wang and Zhou (2021) showed that the challenges faced by ELLs shape their learning outcomes during the acculturation period. The findings of the study indicated that ELLs need to assimilate, integrate into classroom culture, enhance their academic performance, increase self-confidence, and develop their English language communication skills (Wang & Zhou, 2021). Also, Khawaja and Carr's (2020) study revealed that sociocultural support is important for ELLs to integrate successfully into their new learning environment. For instance, Liaqat et al.'s (2021) study supported the idea that ELLs tend to integrate, assimilate, and engage in the new cultural learning environment when they receive social and cultural support from other individuals.

Al-Krenawi et al. (2021) examined the acculturative stress of immigrants enrolled in the United States school settings. The researchers claimed that the acculturation lived experiences of immigrant students in the United States were related to their English language competence, lack of cultural understanding, cultural mistrust, and psychological stress (Al-Krenawi et al., 2021). The researchers noted that acculturative experiences include adapting to a new learning environment, linguistic difficulties, and challenges in assimilating to the host culture environment (Al-Krenawi et al., 2021). Also, the researchers indicated that psychosocial adjustment is an important factor in the immigrant's acculturation lived experiences (Solmaz, 2020). Similarly, Kraus (2023) investigated the acculturative experiences of foreign students. The study has found that assimilation and integration strategies are relevant to the acculturation experiences of foreign students (Kraus, 2023). Al-Krenawi et al.'s (2021) study revealed that immigrants are more likely to acculturate and assimilate into the new cultural learning environment when they have the ability to speak, read, and write the English language. Wei (2021) stated that English language skills are vital for ELLs to linguistically, emotionally, and culturally assimilate to the new cultural learning environment.

Moussa (2021) explored the adaptation of foreign students cross-culturally in the United States and their academic achievement. The study claimed that adaptation to a new cultural learning environment is a challenge because it requires an effective change to the new environment (Moussa, 2021). Also, adaptation to another culture is related to the interest in the host culture, perception of cultural differences, openness, and positivity, which are significant factors that enable ELLs to overcome the challenges they face in the new culture learning environment (Solmaz, 2020). For instance, Castro Olivo et al. (2022) explored a culturally adapted program for ELLs. The researchers claimed that culturally and linguistically diverse students face social and cultural challenges that impact their socialization in U.S. schools (Castro Olivo et al., 2022). ELLs often benefit more when their social, cultural, and emotional learning environment is appropriate and less stressful (Castro Olivo et al., 2022). Also, researchers indicated that linguistic and cultural heritage are important and help ELLs assimilate to the new environment (Lumbrears & Rupley, 2019). However, the researchers claimed that socialization and adaptation to the American school environment represent a huge challenge for ELLs (Lumbrears & Rupley, 2019). According to Moussa (2021), most of the challenges faced by ELLs are related to English language proficiency. For instance, Singer (2022) noted that English language proficiency contributes to ELLs' adaptation to a new learning environment because it enables ELLs to communicate, build new friendships, and accept new cultural traditions. However, the findings of the study revealed that the acculturation and adaptation experiences of the students were horrible: culture shock, sadness, loneliness, and stressful feelings (Björling et al., 2021; Moussa, 2021).

## ELLs Self-Motivation Experiences

Self-motivation is a vital element in the acculturation and academic experiences of ELLs (Sun & Gao, 2020). Sun and Gao (2020) examined the motivation of students. The researchers claimed that motivation is an important factor for positive learning experiences (Sun & Gao, 2020). Researchers noted that students who show interest in a language can improve their communicative abilities tremendously (Sun & Gao, 2020). According to Bedir (2019), ELLs who believe that language ability is innate are more likely to give up compared to ELLs who believe that learning a new language is the result of perseverance and hard work. Therefore, beliefs have the most important effects on the minds of the learners, and beliefs influence ELLs to comprehensively acquire a new language (Bedir, 2019).

Moreover, the perceptions of the learners have a considerable influence on their experiences (Sun & Gao, 2020). Researchers claimed that ELLs' beliefs and attitudes regarding a new language, interest, socialization, and exposure have a great impact on the process by which ELLs acquire a second language (Sun & Gao, 2020). Cho et al. (2020) explored factors that influence the cultural and linguistic needs of ELLs. Researchers believed that ELLs become more involved and willing to take risks when teachers create an enjoyable atmosphere by making classroom environments adequately unpredictable, surprising, and challenging (Cho et al., 2020). Researchers claimed that the more disadvantaged the backgrounds of ELLs, the less likely they are to achieve academic success (Cho et al., 2020).

Motivation veritably impacts ELLs' learning experience (Saito et al., 2018). Students who have a stronger obligation to learn English make unique progress and compress the learning process (Saito et al., 2018). Researchers claimed that ELLs learn better, especially with less anxiety (Rivaz et al., 2019). Researchers indicated that appropriate perceptions also decrease ELLs 'anxieties; they are more comfortable when the learning environment is friendly and pleasant and the teachers encourage them to use the English language without the fear of making errors (Saito et al., 2018). Also, the researcher highlighted the importance of effective motivation and its pedagogical implications for ELLs (Ibrahim, 2023). Ibrahim (2023) found that teachers' perceptions greatly impact ELLs. Research has shown that teachers and students in a classroom can hail from culturally and socially different backgrounds, leading to different perceptions in the classroom setting (Bal, 2022). Additionally, these perceptions influence such an environment, the teachers' decisions, and the learners because perceptions create gaps between teachers and ELLs (Bal, 2022). These differences in perceptions impact ELLs and their achievements as students (Davis &Tesh, 2022; Saito et al., 2018).

Additionally, self-efficacy is an efficacious strategy and an appropriate approach for ELLs (Shi, 2018). Self-efficacy is related to a learner's cognition, emotion, and motivation (Shi, 2018). The researcher claimed that self-efficacy is the notion that the students demonstrate, perceive, and believe in themselves to learn the language (Shi, 2018). Studies have found that ELLs possess the ability to determine their success (Shi, 2018; Sirisha, 2018). According to Wong and Luo (2021), learners achieve higher scores when they have a high degree of self-belief, motivation, and persistence. Also, ELLs face academic challenges, a lack of cultural awareness, learning styles, and social differences concerning their teachers (Wong & Luo, 2021). For instance, these challenges include perceptions, stereotyping, a lack of appropriate academic support, and lower academic performance (Wong & Luo, 2021). Similarly, Camping et al. (2023) claimed that teaching ELLs English as a second language is complex. Additionally, processing a new language can be difficult for many ELLs (Camping et al., 2023). The complexity of language processing can be overcome by implementing the appropriate perceptions and teaching strategies (Camping et al., 2023). The researchers revealed that learners usually like to compare a new language with their native language, which might not always be the best way to learn a new language (Camping et al., 2023; Sirisha, 2018).

## Teachers of ELLs

The teachers' perceptions play an important role in ELLs' learning experiences (Grenz et al., 2023). Grenz et al. (2023) explored the perceptions of teachers toward ELLs' learning experiences. Grenz et al. (2023) found that the teachers' perceptions about ELLs have existed and intensified in the school cultural environment. Also, researchers indicated that teachers' perceptions exist not only about ELLs but also regarding immigrant students (Grenz et al., 2023; Tudy & Gauran-Tudy, 2020). Furthermore, they claimed that, as per the perceptions of their teachers, ELLs perceive and view the world and the culture in which they find themselves (Grenz et al., 2023). Also, Yough et al. (2023) noted that ELLs are more likely to compare themselves to native English-speaking students in order to avoid unwanted perceptions. Researchers claimed that the appropriate perceptions of teachers can increase the performance of ELLs (Yough et al., 2023). According to Adams and Hord (2023), ELLs enjoy their learning processes in a conducive environment when they feel their teachers demonstrate perceptions that promote and develop their self-confidence to achieve academic goals. Researchers stated that teachers need to acknowledge the impacts of their behavior on ELLs and understand their academic needs as well (Li & Jee, 2021). Similarly, the study revealed that teachers who want success for their ELLs must also remain aware of the importance of creating a more welcoming atmosphere, believing that ELLs can reach their dreams as students (Adams & Hord, 2023).

In addition, the researchers asserted that the perceptions and experiences of teachers from elementary, middle, and high school ELLs are similar and have the same outcomes, even though the teachers may speak languages other than English (Szymanski & Lynch, 2020). For instance, teachers who speak another language have the same attitudes, views, expectations, and perceptions about ELLs, unlike their views on English-speaking students (Szymanski & Lynch, 2020). Researchers found that teachers' perceptions about their students' home languages, cultural backgrounds, and social competencies are related to the latter's academic achievements; these elements are represented as a vital aspect regarding the provision of effective educational services designed to meet the needs of the ELLs (Szymanski & Lynch, 2020). Irby et al. (2020) stated that teachers have different expectations and perceptions of their ELLs than of mainstream students. For instance, many teachers perceive that ELLs are responsible for their own failures and achievements (Irby et al., 2020). Researchers have also revealed that teachers' assumptions are related to the lack of awareness about their own worldview as teachers, their experiences, knowledge, and values (Giles & Yazan, 2020). Additionally, teachers create their classrooms based on their own beliefs, which have a greater effect than what they know about the content, lesson plans, or the types of decisions they adopt to meet the needs of their ELLs (Murphy et al., 2019). Also, when teachers believe in the abilities of their students, the latter group tends to fare better in many ways (Murphy et al., 2019). Researchers noted that teachers' beliefs shape their perceptions of the ELLs (Murphy et al., 2019).

Mills et al. (2020) explored linguistically diverse classrooms. ELLs feel better and improve their English proficiency, prepare themselves for the high demands of using English proficiency in real-world interactions, and demonstrate more self-confidence when their teachers show and communicate their confidence in the abilities of their students (Mills et al., 2020). According to Benbaba and Lindner (2023), ELLs displayed more positive attitudes toward English classrooms that create an environment to increase the use of the target language as a means of improving English language proficiency. For instance, ELLs who received positive comments from their teachers feel more comfortable discussing the definitions of unfamiliar words, understanding their assignments, and completing their tasks (Benbaba & Lindner, 2023). Also, the researchers noted that often, ELLs who receive negative comments and realize that their teachers do not believe in their abilities tend to demonstrate more difficulties in communicating and achieving success (Benbaba & Lindner, 2023). However, researchers suggested that learning another language is not a one-size-fits-all policy due to the diversity in students' learning levels and abilities (Roman et al., 2020). Researchers noted that ELLs tend to have more positive attitudes when teachers create a helpful atmosphere and cultivate positive attitudes toward the ELLs in nearly all languages (Mills et al., 2020; Roman et al., 2020).

## Summary

This literature review aimed to gain a meaningful understanding of the acculturation experiences of ELLs and provide a comprehensive framework that supports their lived experiences and academic achievement in the United States. The literature review provided critical evidence that the acculturation experiences of ELLs have some negative consequences on their academic achievement as a growing population in the United States (Bennouna et al., 2021; Hieu, 2023; Hendy & Cuevas, 2020; Hong et al., 2019; Murray, 2020; Shahbazi, 2020). Therefore, it was necessary to explore ELLs' acculturation experiences and academic achievement scores, which are significantly lower in all core subjects (Soland & Sandilos, 2021).

The chapter started with Berry's (1997) acculturation theory. The acculturation theory was used to explore the acculturation experiences of ELLs. Berry's (1997) acculturation theory was appropriate to explore the acculturation, assimilation, and integration of immigrants. Successful assimilation and integration experiences are essential to help ELLs expand their learning abilities and achieve great academic success (Dang et al., 2022; Sousa et al., 2019). Integration is critical for classroom interactions, significantly in helping ELLs overcome their acculturation challenges and increase their classroom integration experiences (Mardian & Nafissi, 2022). Berry's (1997) acculturation framework offers foundational guidelines to address the acculturation experiences of ELLs by culturally creating a classroom environment that embraces diverse experiences (Mardian & Nafissi, 2022; Olds et al., 2021). Therefore, Berry's (1997) acculturation framework provides the most effective strategies that include teaching practices, cultural engagement, home language encouragement, cultural and instructional practices that facilitate learning, as well as collaborative classroom discussions regarding cultural diversity, which enhance the acculturation experiences of the ELLs. Also, the motivation and self-determination theories were reviewed because of foundational and applicational factors regarding motivation and learning. However, the theories were not considered the appropriate theoretical framework to explore the acculturation experiences of ELLs within the classroom learning environment in the United States (Bennouna et al., 2021; Hieu, 2023).

Following the theoretical framework, several themes emerged from the literature review. The themes included English language learners (ELLs), the barriers and challenges encountered by ELLs, language acquisition experiences of ELLs, ELLs testing accommodations experiences, ELLs academic achievement experiences, ELLs' graduation rates experiences, ELLs acculturation experiences, ELLs' classroom assimilation and integration experiences, ELLs self-motivation experiences, and teachers of ELLs.

The review of the literature revealed that ELLs are students whose primary language is not English (Balilah & Archibald, 2022; Kennedy & McLoughlin, 2023; Meng, 2020). ELLs constitute the most important population group among students in United States public schools (Murphy & Torff, 2019; Shahbazi, 2020). The population of ELLs has more difficulty meeting English language proficiency requirements to pass the state exams (Cho et al., 2019; Soland & Sandilos, 2021). Many ELLs lack motivation and self-efficacy, and they often drop out of school (Hong et al., 2019; Soland & Sandilos, 2021). Some of the experiences encountered by ELLs include sadness and loneliness (Hieu, 2023). Also, ELLs face significant acculturative challenges that include language barriers, unfamiliar norms, new school environments, values, belief systems, and a lack of strength to embrace new cultural identities (Bennouna et al., 2021). The acculturation challenges ELLs face often lead to psychosocial issues that affect academic performance, belonging, and risk of dropping out of school and shape inequitable educational outcomes of ELLs (Bennouna et al., 2021; Hieu, 2023).

In Chapter 2, a comprehensive account of the literature review regarding the acculturation experiences and the challenges ELLs face in public schools across the United States was presented. The study included three more chapters that follow this chapter. In Chapter 3, the researcher discussed the qualitative method, descriptive phenomenological research design, semi-structured interviews, and data collection of this study. In Chapter 4, the researcher presented the results of the study. In Chapter 5, the researcher interpreted the study's findings and recommendations for future research to explore the phenomenon of the ELL population in the United States.

# Chapter 3: Research Methodology

The population of ELLs is the fastest-growing group of students in the United States across school settings such as elementary school, middle school, and high school (Gilblom et al., 2022; Shim & Shur, 2018; Watkinson et al., 2022). The ELL population has increased since the last decade (Zhang et al., 2022). ELLs have faced several challenges as students in the United States (Ma & Xia, 2021; Watkinson et al., 2022). The challenges faced by ELLs include the acculturation experiences of assimilating to the new school culture environment, limited English language proficiency, and lower academic achievement (Stark et al., 2021; Watkinson et al., 2022). The problem addressed in this study was the acculturation experiences of ELLs within the classroom learning environment in the United States (Bennouna et al., 2021; Hendy & Cuevas, 2020; Hong et al., 2019; Murray, 2020; Soland & Sandilos, 2021). The purpose of this qualitative, descriptive phenomenological study was to explore the acculturation experiences of ELLs within the classroom learning environment in the United States. Specifically, the study explored the acculturation experiences of ELLs within the classroom learning environment through the teachers' perspectives, who have experience working with ELLs in the Southeastern United States.

In this chapter, the researcher includes a detailed explanation of the research methodology and the research design that were appropriate to address the problem, the purpose, and the research questions of the study. Also, the researcher provides a discussion of the target population and the sample size, as well as the materials, study procedures, data analysis, assumptions, limitations, delimitations, and ethical assurances of the study. Finally, the chapter ends with a summary and an outline of the remaining chapters of the study.

## Research Methodology and Design

The qualitative research design for the study was descriptive phenomenological design. The qualitative method was appropriate to explore the acculturation experiences of ELLs within the classroom learning environment. For instance, a qualitative method is selected when the purpose of the study is to describe human experiences regarding a phenomenon (Creswell, 2014). A qualitative method was also chosen to provide meaningful descriptions of the phenomenon of the study (Maxwell, 2020). The qualitative method provides a unique avenue to describe the challenges faced by ELLs in the classroom in a more meaningful manner that cannot be described by a quantitative method (Hamilton & Finley, 2019; Maxwell, 2020).

Researchers used qualitative methods to explore complex situations and provide meaningful descriptions to understand human phenomena (Maxwell, 2020). Generally, a qualitative study aims to understand and discover the experiences and attitudes of participants by asking questions about a phenomenon (Creswell, 2014). For example, researchers considered a qualitative approach to explore the participants' knowledge, feelings, and perceptions (Creswell, 2014). A qualitative study is associated with questions that seek to identify what and why about participants' perceptions regarding a situation (Creswell, 2014).

On the contrary, researchers indicated that a quantitative method aims to understand the relationships between variables and provide a numerical representation of a population (Hamilton & Finley, 2019; Maxwell, 2020). The quantitative method was not appropriate for the study. For example, a quantitative approach cannot provide meaningful data to describe the acculturation experiences and the challenges faced by ELLs within their classroom learning environment. Instead, a quantitative method aims to generate numerical data (Maxwell, 2020). Therefore, a quantitative method was not considered to meet the purpose of the study (Hamilton & Finley, 2019; Maxwell, 2020).

A qualitative methodology was used to explore the acculturation experiences of ELLs within the classroom learning environment in the United States. A qualitative method is the primary method to truthfully describe and accurately summarize a phenomenon (Anjum et al., 2020; Creswell, 2014). A qualitative method was aligned with the purpose and the research questions of the study. By using a qualitative method, the study provided the richest and the most valuable descriptions regarding the challenges ELLs face in the classroom, which might be used to improve their academic achievement and their acculturation experiences within the classroom learning environment in the United States.

In addition, there are many qualitative research designs (Astroth & Chung, 2018). The qualitative designs include phenomenology, grounded theory, ethnography, narrative, and case study (Astroth & Chung, 2018). A phenomenology design is appropriate when the aim of the study is to identify the experiences and comprehension of the participants, including the researcher's own perceptions of the phenomena (Astroth & Chung, 2018; Watanabe, 2022). For example, the qualitative case design approach is used when the researcher wants to focus on a single case of the phenomenon or a specific subject (Astroth & Chung, 2018). On the other hand, qualitative researchers consider grounded theory when the aim of the study is to develop a theory about the phenomenon of the study (Flynn & Korcuska, 2018). Also, researchers used an ethnographic design, with the aim of the study being to understand a specific situation, group, and culture by observing and looking at documents in a setting (Howson, 2019; Wood & Mattson, 2019). For instance, researchers used a narrative design when the purpose of the study was to share their own stories and retrace historical events (Liestøl, 2019; Nigar, 2020). These qualitative research designs were not aligned with the purpose of the study. Therefore, Giorgi's (2009) descriptive phenomenological design was more appropriate for understanding the acculturation experiences of ELLs within the classroom learning environment in the United States.

The phenomenology approach was originally from Plato, Socrates, and Aristotle (Sabidalas & Esparar, 2022). For instance, Plato and his followers faced challenges in understanding phenomena during their times (Sabidalas & Esparar, 2022). Also, in the 20th century, researchers established a more comprehensive foundational work for understanding human experiences (Sabidalas & Esparar, 2022). The researchers stated that the individual's consciousness is the central factor in the human experience (Sabidalas & Esparar, 2022). Therefore, individuals can describe their experiences (Shorey & Ng, 2022). A descriptive phenomenology study aims to describe the essence of human lived experience (Shorey & Ng, 2022). Also, researchers claimed that humans are free agents and that they are influenced by their social and cultural environment (Shorey & Ng, 2022). According to Creswell (2013), phenomenological design is focused on subjective knowledge regarding the individual's experience to determine and understand the nature of the actual phenomenon. For example, Sabidalas and Esparar (2022) used descriptive phenomenological design to explore individual's lived experiences.

Giorgi's descriptive phenomenological design is based on Husserl's phenomenology model (Jackson et al., 2018). Giorgi's design (2009) provides a comprehensive approach to understanding human's lived experiences. Therefore, Giorgi's (2009) descriptive phenomenological design was selected to understand the acculturation lived experiences of ELLs. The descriptive phenomenological design provides the most valuable descriptions to understand individuals' lived experiences about a phenomenon (Giorgi, 2009). For instance, Giorgi's (2009) descriptive phenomenological design is a rigorous approach; it focuses more on the essence of phenomena and is based on a discovery mode.

Researchers used descriptive phenomenological design to obtain descriptions from participants' perspectives and their lived experiences (O'Brien et al., 2019; Turale, 2020). For example, the descriptive phenomenological design is a comprehensive design, and it provides words that describe the participants' perceptions of the research questions (Koketso et al., 2019). Researchers used descriptive phenomenological design to understand data that included the participants' feelings, perceptions, experiences, and emotions (Koketso et al., 2019). Researchers also explored naturalistic comprehension and investigated human experience using descriptive phenomenological design (O'Brien et al., 2019; Sabidalas & Esparar, 2022).

The descriptive phenomenological design was appropriate, suitable, and powerful for the study (Anjum et al., 2020). The descriptive phenomenological design has less inference, allowing researchers to stay closer to the data (Seixas et al., 2018; Turale, 2020). Therefore, descriptive phenomenological design enables the study participants to fully share their own experiences regarding the challenges ELLs face. Furthermore, Giorgi's (2009) descriptive phenomenological design was aligned with the research questions and the purpose of the study. Giorgi's (2009) descriptive phenomenological design was used to explore the phenomenon of the study.

Describing the phenomenon from individuals' points of view, gathering experiences through their own words, and understanding the meaning of those experiences through semi-structured interviews were appropriate approaches (Giorgi, 2009). Three research questions were used to address the acculturation experiences of ELLs within the classroom learning environment in the United States. The research questions generated rich information by providing words rather than numerical numbers. By describing the acculturation experiences and the challenges faced by ELLs from teachers' perspectives, the findings of this study provide accurate knowledge to understand the challenges faced by ELLs within the classroom learning environment. The results of this study might enable teachers, school administrators, and other school personnel to have a greater understanding and provide more support to meet the needs of ELLs in the United States across school settings.

**Population and Sample**

There was a lack of data about how teachers describe the acculturation experiences faced by ELLs, especially in the Southeastern United States (Garcia-Borrego et al., 2020; Murphy & Torff, 2019). Therefore, this qualitative, descriptive phenomenological study was conducted with public classroom teachers as the appropriate participants and setting for the study. The process of choosing the sample size for the study included the general population, the target population, and the sample size. The number of ELLs in the United States has increased, and there is a need for teachers and others to describe and understand the acculturation experiences and the challenges faced by ELLs within the classroom settings across the country (Murphy & Torff, 2019). Garcia et al. (2019) identified the urgent need to examine ELLs' academic performance. ELLs' sociocultural experiences and academic needs are immense (Garcia et al., 2019; Murphy & Torff, 2019; Szymanski & Lynch, 2020).

The general population for the study included classroom teachers who have experience working with ELLs. ELLs' population has increased by 29% from 2000 to 2016 (Szymanski & Lynch, 2020). The number of ELLs is about 5.5 million in the last 15 years (Shim & Shur, 2018). According to Shim and Shur (2018), by 2025, one in four students in public schools will be an ELL in the United States. Also, ELLs are from different cultural backgrounds (Artigliere, 2019). ELLs have become an issue for teachers and other stakeholders, mainly due to the achievement gaps between ELLs and non-ELL students (Shim & Shur, 2018). Therefore, the study may provide a better understanding of the challenges faced by ELLs in their classroom settings. This study may also influence teachers' guidance counselors' and school administrators' consciousness regarding how they perceive ELLs' acculturation and academic experiences.

The process to determine the target population from the general population was public classroom teachers with experience working with ELLs and teachers with current teacher's certification in the Southeastern United States. Also, teachers who did not have current certification in the Southeastern United States, teachers who did not have experience working with ELLs, and teachers who were not currently working in a public school were excluded from the study. The specific number of years of experience working with ELLs was not counted as a necessary factor for a teacher to participate in the study. The qualitative descriptive phenomenological study did not require a large sample size (Creswell, 2013; Giorgi, 2009). The target population was appropriate for exploring the acculturation experiences of ELLs because teachers have unique lived experiences working with ELLs, and their experiences are relevant to describing the acculturation experiences of ELLs. The classroom teachers were suitable to answer the research questions instead of considering ELLs directly because many ELLs lacked English language proficiency to share their acculturation experiences (Murphy & Torff, 2019).

The sample size in qualitative descriptive phenomenological studies is smaller than in quantitative studies (Creswell, 2013; Giorgi, 2009).

The researchers indicated no straightforward and specific sample size for qualitative studies (Sim et al., 2018; Vasileiou et al., 2018). The sample size in qualitative studies was selected to provide adequate and rich information to meet the purpose of the study (Sim et al., 2018). However, the sample size in qualitative descriptive phenomenological studies must be large enough to provide sufficient data for data saturation and to interpret the phenomenon (Bullard, 2019; Roudsari, 2019). Researchers claimed that saturation is where the data cannot generate new information for the research questions (Vasileiou et al., 2018).

This qualitative descriptive phenomenological study included eight participants. For example, eight participants were enough and provided the essential data in this qualitative descriptive study because the population was homogeneous (Vasileiou et al., 2018). In addition, purposive sampling was selected to provide adequate descriptions of the acculturation experiences of ELLs within the classroom learning environment. Purposive sampling is the strategy that qualitative researchers use to screen the participants who meet the inclusion criteria of the study (Ellis, 2021; Stavropoulou et al., 2022).

The study included the following process: the site authorization from an elementary school and the school district's permission was granted. I met with the school's principal and explained the purpose of the study, the educational implications, and the benefits of the study results. Also, the Institutional Review Board (IRB) approval was solicited and granted from the National University (NU) before any data collection for the study. After the approval from the IRB, the school district's permission, and the site authorization from the school's principal, I pursued the recruitment and data collection process for the study. The recruitment letter was sent to all school teachers through their school emails. The letter included the purpose of the study, the criteria to participate in the study, an informed consent form with all descriptions, explanations, implications of the study, benefits, and information on how to contact me for questions and clarification (see Appendix A). Telephone, email, and Google Meet links were used to communicate with the participants of the study. The participants signed the informed consent form and returned it to ensure their participation in the study. After collecting the informed consent form from the potential participants, the researcher protected all their personal information and avoided the risk of not sharing the personal information of the study participants.

The researcher used the following plans to account for attrition in the qualitative study. Plan A: The researcher recruited a minimum of 10 public school teachers in the southeastern United States. By recruiting participants from the same school area and student demographic, the teachers provided similar descriptions of the challenges faced by ELLs in their classrooms. Plan B: The researcher planned to recruit other teachers from the other schools in the same area. The population of the second school was similar to the primary school's demographic. Plan C: In case of difficulties in recruiting sufficient participants for the study, the researcher developed several plans to extend the location of the study. The plan included another public school that was located in the same area as the primary target school. However, the ELLs' demographics were similar. Therefore, the researcher recruited enough participants and did not use Plans B and C.

## Materials

The study included an interview guide. An interview is a communication between the researcher and the study participants (Kvale, 1996). This conversation has been applied in qualitative studies to explore human phenomena, and interviews are also used in social science studies (Kvale, 1996). Kvale (1996) provided the theoretical foundation for developing interview questions in qualitative studies. According to Kvale (1996), interviews are essential for obtaining an individual's real-life experience. The interview guide was developed to provide a clear direction on the interview questions of the study (see Appendix B).

Semi-structured interviews were suitable for describing the acculturation experience faced by ELLs. Qualitative studies have numerous opportunities to collect data (Belotto, 2018). These sources of data collection include narratives, observations, documents, field notes, questionnaires, interviews, and focus group interviews (Belotto, 2018; Helmich et al., 2018; Shekhar et al., 2019). However, choosing the appropriate data source is vital to exploring and understanding human lived experiences (Helmich et al., 2018; Shekhar et al., 2019). According to Helmich et al. (2018) and Shekhar et al. (2019), semi-structured interviews provide opportunities to ask follow-up questions, enable the participants to clarify their intentions and produce the most meaningful data and fruitful information about the research questions.

The study included seventeen interview questions and seven possible follow-up questions. The interview questions were developed and aligned with the research questions to provide meaningful descriptions of how teachers describe the acculturation experiences of ELLs within the classroom learning environment (see Appendix A). I conducted a field-testing expert to ensure that the semi-structured interview questions were appropriate to provide comprehensive and meaningful data to understand the acculturation experiences of ELLs within the classroom learning environment. The purpose of using field-testing experts was to ensure that the semi-structured interview questions were relevant to maintain trustworthiness in this qualitative descriptive phenomenological study (Creswell, 2013). Trustworthiness includes credibility, dependability, confirmability, and transferability (Lincoln & Guba, 1986). The trustworthiness of a qualitative study depends on the confidence that other researchers place in the process that the current researcher used to collect the data and the careful interpretation of the data to ensure the quality of the study (Lincoln & Guba, 1986). Researchers need to ensure accuracy and maintain trustworthiness in qualitative research (Lincoln & Guba, 1986).

This study's field-testing included three experts with experience with ELLs and qualitative research. I emailed three professors who are experts in the study area, such as ELLs and qualitative studies and asked them to be part of the study's field testing. The interview questions were sent to the experts, and I asked them to provide their feedback regarding whether the interview questions were suitable for meeting the purpose of the study. I reviewed the experts' feedback and made the relevant changes recommended to meet the purpose of the study. Also, the Flesch-Kincaid readability scale was used to ensure the readability of the interview questions. The readability of the informed consent documents was below the 10th-grade level and easy to understand by the study participants.

### Study Procedures

I completed all Collaborative Institutional Training Initiative (CITI) requirements. The IRB approval was solicited and granted from NU before engaging in data collection for the study. Site authorization from the school principal and school district permission were solicited (see Appendix C). After the IRB approval, the school district permission and site authorization from the school principal were granted, and then the researcher began the process of recruiting participants for the study. The researcher provided a copy of the recruitment letter, a copy of the school district permission, and a copy of the IRB final approval to the school principal. Then, the researcher accessed the potential participants through their school email. The researcher sent an invitation to all potential study participants by email, including an attachment of the recruitment letter. The recruitment letter included detailed descriptions, such as the implications of the findings of the study and how the potential participants could contact the researcher of the study. For instance, the recruitment letter included the following key points: The purpose of the study, the criteria to participate in the study, the activities included in this study, how all data in this study were collected, protected, stored, and destroyed by the researcher of this study, and information how to contact the researcher of the study if they were interested in participating in this study.

The participants in the study signed the informed consent form and returned it to the researcher before their participation in the study. The researcher provided an email address and a telephone number to contact the researcher for clarifications and questions about the study. The informed consent form was obtained from the potential participants before the interview. Then, the researcher emailed the potential participants separately and scheduled a day and a time for the individual interviews. Throughout the study, the researcher ensured that the participants voluntarily signed the informed consent form and freely accepted participation. The researcher made all efforts to minimize risks and protect the participants' personal information before and after the study. The researcher obtained the informed consent form and the participants' demographic questionnaire before the interviews. For example, it is required to explain the process of the interviews and ensure that the participants understand the purpose and benefits of the study (Giorgi, 2009). The researcher saved the participants' responses on a USB drive after the transcriptions of the interviews with a coded password. The researcher stored all collected data in the filing cabinet in his home office, which is secured and protected with an alarm system.

The participants of the study completed the demographic questionnaire. The participants received the demographic questionnaire through their emails. The demographic questionnaire included questions about the current grade of teaching experiences, educational credentials, ethnic background, and gender. Also, the demographic questionnaire allowed the participants to describe the current classroom demographics, such as the number of ELLs in their classrooms.

The individual interviews lasted about 27 to 59 minutes. The study did not include multiple interview sessions with the participants. It was not a requirement in this study. However, the participants had an opportunity to review and change their responses during the study's member-checking process. The interviews were conducted during non-contact hours before and after dismissal at a suitable time for each participant. I used Google Meet as an alternative location to conduct these interviews. Researchers indicated that virtual meetings are becoming useful ways to conduct interviews (Flynn et al., 2018).

The interviews were recorded using an electronic device and a Google Meet device. The researcher informed the participants before the recording started, a couple of minutes before the interviews. I reminded the participants that they could stop participating in the study without penalty. The interviews began with an introductory question, and the participants were allowed to share their lived experiences regarding the phenomenon under investigation, which was the acculturation experiences of ELLs within the classroom learning environment. There were more intensive questions with the intent to explore and gather data on the phenomenon of ELLs. The interviews took place in a confidential setting and appropriate atmosphere, as required by Giorgi's (2009) research design.

The study applied a member-checking technique to reinforce credibility. The purpose of member checking was to ensure that the transcription of the interviews represented the participants' descriptions and experiences of the phenomenon (Lincoln & Guba, 1986). According to Lincoln and Guba (1986), member checking is useful for establishing credibility. The researcher of the study sent the transcribed copy of the interviews through the participants' email and requested the participants to check the transcribed interview document for accuracy and ensure that the essence of the lived experience was represented. The participants received a copy of the transcribed interview document within 72 hours after the interview through their email. Member checking technique was used to ensure that the participants' intentions were reflected in their responses (Karimi et al., 2017).

**Data Analysis**

The data analysis in the study followed Giorgi's (2009) descriptive phenomenological data analysis process. The descriptive phenomenological analysis technique provides a meaningful way to describe the lived experience of the participants (Giorgi, 2009). For instance, the aim of Giorgi's (2009) five-step data analysis is to identify the meaning, assess the significance of the meaning, synthesize the meaning, and present the experiences of the participants in the study. The lived experiences can be understood by acquiring qualitative data as a whole scientific investigation, which is referred to as bracketing to interpret the meanings and essences of the individual's experience (Giorgi, 2009).

The goal of using the phenomenological data analysis process is to approach the data with a phenomenological scientific reduction attitude and a psychological attitude and to develop a sensitivity to the phenomenon under investigation (Giorgi, 2009). Therefore, Giorgi's (2009) data analysis steps were appropriate strategies to provide meaningful descriptions of the phenomenon. Phenomenological data analysis enables researchers to focus on the patterns that capture the participants' experiences in a meaningful way that answers the study's research questions (Castleberry & Nolen, 2018; Jones et al., 2018). Phenomenological data analysis is suitable when researchers want to explore the participants' experiences directly, accurately, and truthfully (Filia et al., 2018; Scharp & Sanders, 2019). Before the data analysis of the study, the documents were secured and protected with a password on a USB. The participants' identifications were removed, and the confidentiality was maintained. The data were reviewed to ensure the information was relevant for the inductive data analysis process.

The first step of Giorgi's (2009) analysis model is initial reading for a sense of the whole. Giorgi (2009) asks the researcher to familiarize himself with the data as a whole. During step one, the researcher familiarized himself with the data by listening to the audio-recorded interviews and transcribed them into a Word document. Then, the next phase was to gain initial knowledge of the data, which was a tentative understanding of the participant's whole sense of descriptive account regarding the phenomenon (Giorgi, 2009). The document for each participant included an identifier. After familiarizing them with the data, the following procedure was to read the data and search for meaning and patterns in the entire data before the next step.

The second step of Giorgi's (2009) analysis method was adopting the phenomenological and psychological attitude or delineating meaning units. The second step involves two elements of Giorgi's (2009) data analysis: the natural attitude and the phenomenological psychological reduction of the study's researcher. The aim of this step was to search for meaning units by marking relevant information and highlighting the important words and sentences relative to the study's purpose and the research questions.

The third step of Giorgi's (2009) analysis model was dividing the data into meaning units or transforming the units into expressions of meanings. The main goal of this step was to break down the descriptive material into smaller, manageable units and distinguish the participants' meanings. However, the meaning units may include words, sentences, and paragraphs (Giorgi, 2009). There were two columns. For instance, the left column included the descriptive material, and the right column contained the meaning units.

The fourth step of Giorgi's (2009) analysis model was transforming everyday expressions into psychological meaning or crafting the informed meaning structure. For example, the search in this step was to find the general meanings within the participant's lived experiences (Giorgi, 2009). Therefore, the focus was on the acculturation experiences of ELLs within the classroom learning environment by allowing the psychologically relevant meanings to emerge through the participants' own expressions (Giorgi, 2009). For example, the role of the researcher was to summarize the psychologically relevant meanings of one's consciousness (Giorgi, 2009).

The last step of Giorgi's (2009) analysis model focused on the constituents that emerged from the phenomenon. The relevant structure of participants' experiences of the phenomenon was written, and the acculturation experiences of ELLs within the classroom learning environment were presented. Finally, the phenomenological stance of the study was that the data analysis conducted and presented the essential structure of the phenomenon (Åhs et al., 2023; Donate et al., 2021; Hansson et al., 2022; Rodriguez et al., 2019).

### Assumptions

The primary assumption in the study was that the qualitative descriptive phenomenological design included the sources of data and the data analysis approach, which were appropriate methods to describe the phenomenon of the study (Castleberry & Nolen, 2018; Turale, 2020). The second assumption of the study was that the participants provided honest and accurate interview responses (Turale, 2020). Additionally, the researcher assumed that participants truthfully completed the demographic questionnaire, given the ethical considerations and guaranteed confidentiality in this study (Castleberry & Nolen, 2018; Turale, 2020). The researcher assumed that the findings of the study might be useful to reeducate school leaders about the challenges faced by ELLs within the classroom learning environment, enhance their acculturation experiences, motivate ELLs to strive and improve their academic achievement and close the gap that exists between ELLs and non-ELL students in the United States.

## Limitations

Limitations are factors over which the researcher has no control (Theofanidis & Fountouki, 2018). The study included several limitations. The first limitation was self-reported data, which included the demographic questionnaire and semi-structured interviews. The researcher used a member-checking process to improve the study's trustworthiness. For instance, to mitigate this limitation, the researcher created an appropriate environment and believed that the participants' descriptions of the acculturation experience of ELLs in the classroom learning environment were meaningful and accurate.

The second limitation of the study is that this qualitative study aimed to be an in-depth exploration of ELLs' acculturation experiences through teachers who have experience working with ELLs. The believability of the data was limited because it was through the eyes of the teachers and not necessarily through the eyes of ELLs. Therefore, the findings were limited to that population. The third limitation of the study was the demographic and geographical location. The ELL population included students from diverse cultural backgrounds. The participants may not have direct experiences with all students who compose the population of ELLs. The participants may lack cultural awareness to describe the relevant challenges faced by ELLs. Therefore, the participants' descriptions of the phenomenon may not be consistent with other groups of ELLs due to the socioeconomic, sociocultural, and geographical components of the ELL population. To mitigate this limitation, the researcher can increase the sample size and conduct this study in another region of the country.

## Delimitations

Delimitations are factors in the researcher's control (Theofanidis & Fountouki, 2018). The qualitative descriptive phenomenological study included several delimitations. One of the delimitations of the study was that the participants were current certified public classroom teachers. The teachers in the Southeastern United States who have experience working with ELLs. Additionally, the study included a methodological delimitation. For example, quantitative methods aim to understand the relationships between variables (Hamilton & Finley, 2019; Maxwell, 2020). On the contrary, qualitative methods aim to discover, understand, describe, and explore the participants' attitudes, views, knowledge, feelings, and experiences in natural settings (Hamilton & Finley, 2019; Maxwell, 2020). A qualitative descriptive phenomenological design was appropriate to describe the challenges faced by ELLs (Astroth & Chung, 2018).

**Ethical Assurances**

I ensured that ethical considerations remained a priority throughout the study process. The IRB approval was granted before the data collection process. In addition, I contacted the school district in the area for permission and a school principal for site authorization in the Southeastern United States. After obtaining the permission and the site authorization, I started the process of recruitment. I provided the informed consent form to the target participants who agreed to voluntarily participate in the study. I emailed the potential participants of the study. The email included the recruitment letter and informed consent form. After collecting the signed informed consent from the participants, the process of data collection began by conducting semi-structured individual interviews and completing the demographic questionnaire.

The research indicated that whenever human subjects are the participants in a study, the researcher needs to consider the potential ethical risks (McGregor & Tsosie, 2021). The Belmont Reports in 1979 required researchers to address ethical principles as to human persons (McGregor & Tsosie, 2021). The ethical principles of the Belmont Reports in 1976 highlighted the need for researchers to have respect for persons, beneficence, and justice (McGregor & Tsosie, 2021). The ethical principles require researchers to take necessary steps to be fair, to protect, and to do no harm to human subjects (McGregor & Tsosie, 2021). However, the ethical risk in the study was minimal. I took all necessary precautions to address ethical issues with the participants and inform them of any danger, such as describing an experience that may be traumatic. However, after the interviews, the participants were happy to participate in this study. Also, they did not share any complaints about their participation in the study. To address any potential risk, such as confidentiality and to protect participants' privacy, I provided an identifier, such as P1-P8, to each participant interview's transcript. My duty was to avoid any risk of revealing any information to the public that may impact participants' careers and the credibility of the study. Researchers stated that confidentiality is a crucial factor in a research study (McGregor & Tsosie, 2021). I emphasized the importance of the informed consent form. Also, I ensured that the participants fully understood and freely gave their consent to participate voluntarily in the study.

The participants were informed of the benefits and any risks that could be expected regarding the procedure. Before the interviews, the participants knew that they could withdraw from the study at any time and that there would be no penalty. Also, I informed the participants that the findings of the study belonged to the researcher. I ensured that the participants' privacy and information were maintained. Therefore, I protected the data of this study by keeping all the interview transcripts with the participant's identifier in a locked file cabinet in my office. One of the significant responsibilities was to make sure that the information of the participants was protected during and after the study. I coded the data to avoid any relevant information from being revealed to the public and to protect the identity of each participant. The dissertation chair and IRB may have access to the study's data. I mitigated the impact of social desirability bias during and after the study. The plan is to maintain all recorded materials and documents in a private file cabinet for three years. After that, the data and recorded materials will be destroyed by cutting and shredding them into pieces.

## Summary

The chapter included the research methodology and the research design of the study. A qualitative descriptive phenomenological design was appropriate to explore the acculturation experiences of ELLs within the classroom learning environment. A qualitative method was adopted in the study because the qualitative method provides a true representation, a deep, rich, and detailed meaningful description of the phenomenon (Cömert, 2018; Hamilton & Finley, 2019; Maxwell, 2020). The study participants were eight elementary classroom teachers. The participants provided the most meaningful descriptions regarding the acculturation experiences faced by ELLs within the classroom learning environment in the Southeastern United States. Giorgi's (2009) data analysis approach was selected to describe words, phrases, quotes, and meaning units from teachers' perspectives about the acculturation challenges ELLs face. The chapter highlighted the assumptions, limitations, delimitations, and ethical assurances of the study and the chapter summary. In Chapter 4, I discussed the results of the study. In Chapter 5, I interpreted the study's findings, and I made recommendations for future research regarding the phenomenon of the study.

The problem addressed by this study was the acculturation experiences of ELLs within the classroom learning environment in the United States (Bennouna et al., 2021; Hendy & Cuevas, 2020; Hong et al., 2019; Murray, 2020; Soland & Sandilos, 2021). The purpose of this qualitative, descriptive phenomenological study was to explore the acculturation experiences of ELLs within the classroom learning environment in the United States. The acculturation experiences are considered some of the significant challenges faced by English language learners (ELLs) within the classroom learning environment in the United States. ELLs are from different countries (Garcia-Borrego et al., 2020).

Also, the English language is not the primary language of ELLs (Garcia-Borrego et al., 2020; Watkinson et al., 2022). Researchers indicated that the population of ELLs is the fastest-growing group of students in the United States across K-12th grade school settings such as elementary school, middle school, and high school (Gilblom et al., 2022; Shim & Shur, 2018; Watkinson et al., 2022). The ELL population in the United States has constantly and rapidly increased since the last decade (Zhang et al., 2022). The researchers found that the population of students in the United States has become more diverse (Johnson & Thorne-Wallington, 2021). The population of ELLs in public schools in the United States was about 5 million students in 2000 (Zhang et al., 2022). There was a need to address the acculturation experiences of ELLs within the classroom learning environment. Therefore, three research questions guided the study.

**Research Question 1**

What are teachers' lived experiences of the acculturation faced by ELLs within the classroom learning environment in the United States?

**Research Question 2**

What are teachers' lived experiences addressing the acculturation of ELLs within the classroom learning environment in the United States?

**Research Question 3**

What are the strategies that teachers use to address the acculturation experiences of ELLs within the classroom learning environment in the United States?

This chapter provides a review of the trustworthiness of the data collected from the study participants. The participants were public school teachers in the Southeastern United States. The chapter also presents the findings of the study. The findings are presented on the research questions and constituents of the study. The findings were also evaluated through the lens of the research questions, the literature review, and the study's theoretical framework. This chapter ended with a summary of the essential key points covered in the chapter and led to the next chapter of the study.

## Trustworthiness of the Data

Trustworthiness in this descriptive phenomenological study included credibility, dependability, confirmability, and transferability (Lincoln & Guba, 1986). The trustworthiness of a qualitative study depends on the confidence that other researchers place in the process that the current researcher used to collect the data and the careful interpretation of the data to ensure the quality of the study (Guba, 1981). Researchers must ensure accuracy and trustworthiness in qualitative research (Lincoln & Guba, 1986). Researchers must act responsibly and ethically during the entire research process (Lincoln & Guba, 1986). The crucial part of this study was to describe the challenges of ELLs and present the findings of this study in a way that other researchers can trust, follow the same steps, and expect to find equivalent results (Lincoln & Guba, 1986).

### *Credibility*

Credibility refers to the notion that data from participants' intentions and representations are true (Amankwaa, 2016). The credibility of a study is established when the researcher generates accurate and truthful data from the participants' experiences and views (Amankwaa, 2016). The researcher considered that credibility is the process that the data collection, data analysis, and findings are valuable and believable, offering a guarantee to the readers and audiences regarding the phenomenon (Amankwaa, 2016).

I ensured the credibility plan was well executed and documented during the process of data collection and data analysis in this study. The credibility of this study included the following steps. First, semi-structured interviews and a demographic questionnaire were used to allow the participants to describe their experiences with ELLs in the Southeastern United States. Second, the interview questions were evaluated by a panel of three experts. The field testing was conducted to ensure that the data collection plan was valuable enough to meet the purpose of the study. Third, I ensured that the interpretation and representation of the participants reflected their views. The researcher well documented and achieved the data plan of this study. I applied a member-checking process to reinforce the credibility of this qualitative descriptive phenomenological study. According to Lincoln and Guba (1986), member-checking is a useful technique for establishing credibility. The data of this qualitative descriptive phenomenological study were saturated after eight meaningful interviews. Researchers claimed that saturation is the point where the data cannot generate any new information for the research questions (Vasileiou et al., 2018).

### Dependability

Dependability refers to the notion that the findings are consistent and the findings could be related to similar conditions (Lincoln & Guba, 1986). Additionally, dependability in qualitative studies refers to the concept that the findings of the study are not influenced by the researcher's interests and biases, but the findings are truly from the participants' views of the phenomenon (Soroush et al., 2018). The dependability of this qualitative study included the details that future researchers can follow to repeat the same data collection, data analysis, interview process, and findings interpretation process. I established the dependability of the data by using Giorgi's (2009) analysis techniques to create patterns, meaning units, and constituents that were consistent with the participants' meaningful expressions and understanding of the phenomenon. Additionally, the findings of this study can be replicated under the same conditions if other researchers follow the same techniques and procedures of the entire study. Also, the dependability of this study included the interviews being transcribed and followed by members checking for accuracy. The methodological descriptions of this study included data collection, data analysis, the IRB process, school district approval, and site authorization.

### *Transferability*

Transferability refers to the notion that the findings of the study apply to other groups and similar settings (Amankwaa, 2016). Also, transferability refers to the notion that the steps of a study can be replicated and applied by other researchers (Castleberry & Nolen, 2018). The researcher indicated that transferability in qualitative research enables other researchers to follow the same steps to produce insightful results (Castleberry & Nolen, 2018). The results and findings of this study could be applied to future research. Future researchers may be able to replicate this study by following the same population, sample size, method, research design, and sources of data; then, under the same conditions, the results may be similar. Also, transferability in this study included sampling sufficiency and thick descriptions. In this study, sampling sufficiency included eight public classroom teachers in the Southeastern United States. This sample was appropriate and provided meaningful descriptions of how teachers describe the acculturation experiences of ELLs within the classroom learning environment in the Southeastern United States. This study provided relevant information about the acculturation experiences of ELLs. The researcher of this study considered that the findings might influence other researchers to further explore the acculturation experiences of ELLs in the United States.

### *Confirmability*

Confirmability refers to the notion that the researcher of the study demonstrates a degree of neutrality and that the findings represent the participants' intentions (Amankwaa, 2016). Also, confirmability in the qualitative descriptive study included that the findings are accurate, meaningful, and accepted by others (Soroush et al., 2018). Researchers indicated that confirmability existed when the results of the study reflected and represented the participants' true experiences as well as being free from the investigator's biases and preferences (Lincoln & Guba, 1986). In this study, the researcher demonstrated confirmability by ensuring that the data represented the participants' experiences and viewpoints of the phenomenon (Lincoln & Guba, 1986). The researcher presented the participants' descriptive views of the acculturation experiences of ELLs without bias. The researcher developed the interview questions. A panel of three experts reviewed the interview questions to ensure that these questions were suitable to provide accurate and valuable data to meet the purpose of this study. The interview transcripts were followed by members checking for the accuracy of the participants' views (Lincoln & Guba, 1986).

**Reflexivity**

My personal experiences as an immigrant, an ELL, a father of two ELLs, a former community language facilitator (CLF), and a currently certified guidance counselor in the Southeastern United States were the unique reasons for conducting this qualitative descriptive phenomenological study. The research process may be influenced by the researcher's personal experiences (Åhs et al., 2023; Donate et al., 2021; Hansson et al., 2022; Rodriguez et al., 2019). I witnessed my own children struggle as ELLs. I also have my own experiences as an ELL, where I did not know how to describe and address the difficulties I faced and the challenges my children and other ELLs experienced besides encouraging them to study harder. There was a need to bring awareness of how teachers can be properly trained to teach ELLs and develop sensitivity awareness toward ELLs to make their acculturation experiences within the classroom learning environment innovative and successful.

I have learned that the dissertation process is an interactive process that requires the learner to maintain an open-minded perspective. It is an opportunity to learn and apply what is learned throughout the process. As the researcher, the learner needs to prepare academically and psychologically because the dissertation process is very challenging. The dissertation process is not a straightforward process. There are surprises. Learners need to prepare for that and be willing to make changes and corrections throughout the process. I believe that there is no easy step or phase during the dissertation process because each phase has its own challenges and surprises that require the learner to show a willingness to move forward in the process.

## Results

This qualitative descriptive phenomenological study filled a gap regarding the acculturation experiences of ELLs within the classroom learning environment in the United States. Data saturation was reached after eight meaningful interviews. The interviews were conducted through Google Meet. The interviews lasted between 27 and 59 minutes. Giorgi's (2009) five-step data analysis process guided this qualitative descriptive phenomenological study. The first step of Giorgi's (2009) data analysis model is an initial reading for a sense of the whole. The researcher was able to familiarize himself with the data as a whole. I was able to gain the initial knowledge of the data, which was a tentative understanding of the phenomenon of the study (Giorgi, 2009). The second step of Giorgi's (2009) data analysis method is the phenomeno-logical and psychological attitude or delineating meaning units. I gained a natural attitude and phenomenological and psychological reduction. I marked and highlighted some key words, sentences, and paragraphs that were relevant to the acculturation experiences of ELLs, the purpose of the study, and the research questions.

The third step of Giorgi's (2009) data analysis is transforming the meaning units. I transformed the descriptive material into smaller, manageable units and distinguished the participants' meanings. However, the meaning units included words, sentences, and paragraphs (Giorgi, 2009). The fourth step of Giorgi's (2009) data analysis model is the transformation of everyday expression into psychological meaning. For example, the search in this step was to find the general meanings within the participants' lived experience (Giorgi, 2009). Therefore, the focus was on the acculturation experiences of ELLs within the classroom learning environment by allowing the psychologically relevant meanings to emerge through the participants' expressions (Giorgi, 2009). For example, the role of the researcher was to summarize the psychologically relevant meanings of one's consciousness (Giorgi, 2009). The last step of Giorgi's (2009) data analysis model is to form the constituents that are the essential structure of the phenomenon.

The relevant structure of the participants' experiences of the phenomenon was written and presented the acculturation experiences of ELLs within the classroom learning environment (Åhs et al., 2023; Donate et al., 2021). After the data analysis process, nine meaningful constituents related to teachers' descriptions of the acculturation experiences of ELLs emerged. Four of the constituents emerged in response to Research Question 1, two of the constituents addressed Research Question 2, and three of the constituents addressed Research Question 3. The following section provides detailed information on each participant in the study.

### Participant Demographics

Table 1 indicates the participants' demographic information, including pseudonyms, gender, education, ethnicity, years of teaching ELLs, and current grade of teaching. A diverse group of participants described their experiences regarding the acculturation experiences of ELLs within the classroom learning environment in the Southeastern United States.

| Pseudonym | Gender | Education | Ethnicity | Years of Teaching of ELLs | Grade of Teaching |
|---|---|---|---|---|---|
| P1 | F | Master | Asia | 21 | Third |
| P2 | F | Master | Haitian American | 8 | Third |
| P3 | F | Master | Haitian American | 7 | Fourth |
| P4 | F | Bachelor | White | 4 | Second |
| P5 | M | Master | Jamaican | 8 | Fifth |
| P6 | F | Bachelor | Italian | 10 | Fourth |
| P7 | F | Bachelor | Spanish | 35 | Kindergarten |
| P8 | F | Master | African-American | 21 | Fifth |

***Table 1.*** *Participant Demographics*

### *Participant Conceptualizations of the Acculturation Experiences of ELLs Within the Classroom Learning Environment*

During the semi-structured interviews, the participants described the acculturation experiences of ELLs. Then, the semi-structured interviews were transcribed using a Google Meet device. Also, member-checking was applied to ensure the accuracy of the participants' descriptions of the phenomenon of the study. The data analysis was guided by Giorgi's (2009) data analysis process. The words, sentences, and paragraphs of the participants' experiences revealed meaningful descriptions regarding the phenomenon investigated by this study (Giorgi, 2009). The phenomenological structures of the participants' experiences were created and transformed into meaning units, constituents, and general structures. The researcher divided the words, sentences, and paragraphs and created the appropriate and relevant constituents that represented the essential structure of the phenomenon.

### *Research Question 1. What Are Teachers' Lived Experiences of the Acculturation Faced by ELLs Within the Classroom Learning Environment in the United States?*

The purpose of this research question was to describe the acculturation experiences of ELLs within the classroom learning environments in the United States from teachers' perspectives. Through several interview questions, the participants in the study described the acculturation experiences of ELLs within the classroom. All of the participants in the study shared a pattern of acculturation experiences of ELLs. The participants' interview transcripts revealed a series of meaningful words, quotes, and paragraphs regarding the lived experiences of ELLs within the classroom learning environments in the United States. Research Question 1 included eight interview questions and three follow-up questions. Also, the data analysis of the study was guided by Giorgi's (2009) five-step data analysis process. At the end of the data analysis process, several meaningful constituents emerged in response to Research Question 1. Table 2 highlights the constituents.

| Constituent | Total of participants |
|---|---|
| 1.  ELLs disconnected from the classroom | 8 |
| 2.  English language barriers faced by ELLs | 8 |
| 3.  Academic disadvantages faced by ELLs within the classroom | 8 |
| 4.  The challenges faced by ELLs to cope within the classroom | 8 |

*Table 2.* Constituents Describing Teachers' Experiences of the Acculturation of ELLs

**Constituent 1. ELLs Disconnected from the Classroom.** All participants described the acculturation experiences faced by ELLs within the classroom environment. The aim of this constituent is to provide a meaningful description of teachers' acculturation experiences faced by ELLs within the classroom environment at the beginning of their acculturation experiences. P2 noticed that ELLs are "Disconnected" at the beginning of acclimating to the new classroom learning environment. P2 stated,

In the beginning, they tend to be shyer and quieter. ELLs struggle a lot, especially in the classroom. They become more reserved. They do not participate as much. They have a little difficulty in making new friends. ELLs face language challenges. When you're talking to them, they have a hard time explaining themselves or communicating with you. So, they are... crying... they're just having a hard time in the classroom.

But as time goes on... they see other peers who probably speak the same language and have the same culture... and they start to participate more. They start to have more confidence in themselves.

P2 also indicated ELLs acculturate to their classroom when the teacher provides a suitable environment for them. For instance, P2 noted, "I've experienced that if you set up a great environment for them, they tend to do better." In addition, P1 stated, "I've taught students from many countries... from China, from Asia such as Japan, Central Asia, and South America." Also, some of the ELLs are children of migrant farm-workers to children who are refugees from Africa." P1 stated, "When they first arrive in the United States, the number one challenge ELLs face is behavior." P1 described, "ELLs have to learn how to follow the rules… in the classroom, and certain expectations may differ from their countries." In addition, P1 noted, "ELLs become Americanized… within a year or two years. They get used to that [*classroom culture*] easily." On the other hand, P3 indicated, "My experiences are with students from a Spanish-speaking background and Haitian Creole background." For instance, to elaborate on the issue, P3 made a comparison between ELLs who have a Spanish cultural background and ELLs who have a Haitian cultural background. P3 stated,

> "My students who have a Spanish cultural background are usually more intimidated… They… participate… as they become more comfortable with the language. But for students who are Haitians, I've noticed they are usually more likely… to engage in the lesson, even if they respond to my questions in their first language… They try to respond to me in Haitian Creole."

For instance, P3 indicated, "They struggle with vocabulary words. They have struggled to ask for help. They… get a little bit quiet and reserved. They take a step back… before they decide to join the class. So, the environment… allows them to… assimilate into the academic culture a little bit faster." Similar to P1, P2, P3, and P4, observed that ELLs face challenges to acculturate to the classroom environment when they arrive in the United States. For instance, P4 described,

> "Typically, what I have experienced here, the students [*ELLs*] for a couple of months, they're in a period of unknown. They're very quiet. They're not talking. They're just kind of a little bit lost. The children [*ELLs*] just were confused. They are trying to fill in… within the environment. I feel that period can last about three months. They pretty much assimilate within the school's culture or the culture around them. So, I feel that socially, they do a great job of assimilating into their environment within the first three-month period. After that, they feel comfortable, and they get to know their teacher. They… assimilate… and adapt themselves to the environment."

P5 viewed teaching ELLs as a "life-changing" experience. Also, P5 described the experiences faced by ELLs, "opened my eyes to… it helps me to remember coming into a different country where you don't know anyone, and you're trying to… assimilate yourself and find out where you belong." P5 also observed ELLs, "facial expressions and their body language. They look lonely." P5 indicated, "The biggest [*challenge*] is the language barrier when they do not understand the language, and it makes it very hard to communicate verbally." In addition, P6 had similar experiences with ELLs. P6 stated, "Most of my kids [*ELLs*] are from Haiti or have parents… from Haiti. I also have students who are from Guatemala… Japan and… from Nicaragua." On the other hand, P8 described that some of her ELLs have a Southeast Asia cultural background. For instance, P8 indicated, "My ELL students maintain their Southeast Asian dishes [*cultural background*]." For instance, P6 shared,

"I have a new girl who just came here three days ago. She did not speak one word of English. She was lost. She looked a little in fear… she was very scared. She didn't even talk to me. The body language… she didn't want to do anything… It's hard for them when they come here. This is how you're in a whole new world. It's not just a new country. It's a new school. They look frustrated, they'll put their head down, they'll cover their head with their hood. They're much quieter; they're much more unlikely to ask for help. It's hard for them to focus on what I know with ELL students. They shut down; some of them become angry, some become upset and emotionally shut down. They disconnect with certain things. They do not have that background in the figurative language. I've had a few students in the past that have gotten very frustrated when they continuously got questions wrong."

For instance, P7 and P8 described different perspectives on the acculturation experiences faced by ELLs within the classroom. P7 shared, "I think that the younger children in kindergarten… they adjust because they're very young. They have positive experiences at a young age. They are very friendly and sociable. They want to socialize with their peers."

Also, P8 emphasized on the economic aspect and its impacts on the acculturation experiences of ELLs. P8 noticed that,

> "It depends on the economic… experience they have here in the United States. So those who come with money have a different experience than those who come with nothing. So, I've noticed some of them can catch on fast, and some of them can't catch it [acculturate] fast because all the resources are not in place. So, they're really quiet. They… stay in their cells. They don't get comfortable with the classroom. Maybe three to four weeks before they become comfortable enough to start talking because they don't know the native language."

**Constituent 2. English Language Barriers Faced by ELLs.** The English language barriers are another constituent that emerged from the participants' meaningful descriptions. All participants of the study noticed that one of the challenges ELLs faced within the classroom learning environment was the English language barrier. The English language barriers have impacted the acculturation experiences of ELLs. For instance, P1 stated, "Okay, I think … when they come to the United States, the number one struggle is learning English as a second language or third language." P2 also indicated,

> "It's the barriers of the two different cultures… they don't understand what's going on in the classroom. It's so different from what they're used to. They do not participate as much, and they tend not to complete their assignments. They don't get much done at all because they don't understand. They struggle… not being able to adapt to the new environment."

P3 also described the challenges faced by ELLs within the classroom learning environment, including the English language barrier. P3 shared that,

> "The lack of vocabulary… is the main struggle. I can tell… they want to ask questions about something as simple as, can I use the bathroom, drink water? They don't know those specific words in English. Even if…

the grammar is incorrect, I can usually tell what they need if they say something like a bathroom or thirsty or pencil or whatever. So, once they... learn those vocabulary words, I can help them along even if they can't... phrase the question accurately at the moment."

In addition, P5 expressed the same experience regarding the English language barriers ELLs face within the classroom learning environment. For instance, P5 stated,

"I think about the struggle... several factors that can cause the struggle. I would say the language barrier. It's obviously the most important. Communicating in a new language is very difficult. It can really hinder their ability to engage and to learn the new culture. They have educational challenges... the kids [*ELLs*] have to take a test in English when they do not... know how to fully read yet in English."

The English language barrier represented one of the major challenges for the population of ELLs. For example, P4, P6, P7, and P8 shared their experiences with ELLs. P4 noticed, "They don't speak unless the other students try to play with them. They stay away... haven't participated. They have a hard time assimilating within the classroom culture." Also, P6 stated,

"I think the biggest thing that I've seen is the language barrier. They are not able to talk to me. I'm very lucky that we have a lot of students who speak their language. So, I didn't have that in my old school. There were very few ELL students. But here, I have plenty of students who can help. But language is very hard to teach someone."

For instance, P7 described,

"They face the language barrier. They don't have the vocabulary words to make this transition easier. They pick up a lot of words through social interactions... with their peers and their classmates. Some of them are shy. It takes time to feel safe or feel comfortable to start interacting with other kids. So, they do need some time."

Similarly to P4, P6, and P7, P8 described,

"A lot of times, professional teachers have a hard time deciding if it's a language barrier or if it is a disability... Sometimes, they're quick to go to school-based teams instead of understanding... they need at least two years to grasp the language... to acclimate to the current world or the current culture."

Therefore, all participants of the study described that one of the acculturation challenges faced by ELLs within the classroom learning environment is the English language barrier. Teachers and ELLs struggle to communicate and that makes it harder for ELLs to acclimate to the new cultural learning environment. The next constituent describes the academic achievement faced by ELLs while they strive to acculturate to the new educational setting.

**Constituent 3. Academic Disadvantages Faced by ELLs Within the Classroom.** All participants were asked to describe the academic experiences faced by ELLs while they assimilated to a new classroom environment in the United States. The participants of the study provided meaningful descriptions of the academic performance of ELLs. For instance, P1 stated, "The ELLs have a bigger load. They have to learn a new language. They have to learn how to adapt to the new environment. So, they have an extra burden compared to native English speakers." P1 also indicated that such experiences have "Affected their academic career in the United States. They need to acculturate to become successful academically. If they are planning to grow up in America, so this is something they have to become successful students."

P5 described some of the challenges that impacted ELLs' academic achievement within the educational setting in the United States. P5 also noticed that academic achievement is not the same for all ELLs. For instance, P5 stated,

"They're being tested in reading, and they must read a couple of paragraphs in English. They are still learning the English language. They are already at a disadvantage...academically. They are really struggled because they're being tested in something that they're not able to do. They struggle academically due to their language barrier, which can then impact their social and emotional being. Some of the ELLs do well, and some don't... I would say the majority of ELLs tend to do well once they feel safe when they start to verbalize more."

Similarly, P6 shared a mix of results of the academic achievement of ELLs within the educational setting. She stated,

"I think they struggle. Almost all my ELL students when they first came, they struggled. Now some of them do make it once they learn the language or start learning the language. There's a girl that came here. I think last year in April. You would never know today she has not been here even one year, which to me is amazing. She can fully speak English. She does her work. She wants to learn. She loves to learn so that's a big thing. She's learning so quickly."

In addition, P7 noticed that the learning pace is too fast for ELLs. She indicated that,

"They are not on the grade level. The content that is being taught, for example, math words plus and minus,... vocabulary words, natural science... precipitation, weather, movement, and push and pull movements, can be frustrating for them so that they don't know these things. Eventually, they will, but that's going to come in time. So, they work independently; they need that support, and they are not able to do that on their own. So, they need support to do well academically. The academics or the curriculums that have been taught to them are the fast pace."

In addition, P2, P3, P4, and P8 described the academic achievement of ELLs within the classroom learning environment. For instance, P2 stated,

It's two different things. One is that if the children were in school before coming to America... I noticed that they do much better than those students who had very little schooling back home... They know the structure. They're able to easily adapt... they tend to do a little better academically. They may score lower than the other kids. However, they tend to show growth over time. Kids who have no schooling tend to struggle a lot academically, and you will see a very slow, steady increase in their academics.

P3 stated that some of the lessons are difficult for ELLs to understand. She indicated that

"So... more in-depth... the lessons have a little bit higher academic rigor... for ELLs to understand the standard." But P3 acknowledged that ELLs struggle academically due to the language barrier. However, She described "But my grades aren't based on test scores. So, I mainly keep track of their progress by... their participation and even if they're getting the questions wrong. I'm not going to score them the lowest... they were trying their best."

P4 emphasized on the experiences of ELLs that impacted their academic achievement within the classroom environment. P4 described that,

"I think we have to remember these are children who are not only learning in a new academic system. They're learning a new language. They're learning a new way of living. They lack the foundational skills or the language to really explain and talk to their teacher... It's crucial because if they don't overcome it, then that can lead to more academic challenges for them ahead. For example, I think about a first grade who had a terrible situation that occurred at the beginning of the school year. She slept throughout the day... which affected her academically."

P8, P5, P7, and P2 shared similar descriptions regarding the academic achievement of ELLs. For instance, P8 indicated that some of the academic challenges faced by ELLs are

"Because some of them never went to school when they were in their native country. They come... they're kind of fearful a little bit. Language plays a big role. It's very hard to communicate when you don't speak the native tongue... So, those struggles within the classroom can be a problem... unfortunately."

All participants in the study described the academic achievement of ELLs. The participants stated that the lack of prior school experiences, the English language barrier, and the inclusion of the new classroom culture environment impacted the academic achievement of ELLs. The next constituent describes the experiences of ELLs coping within the classroom environment.

**Constituent 4. The Challenges Faced by ELLs to Cope Within the Classroom.** All participants of the study shared the acculturation experiences of ELLs coping within the classroom environment. P4 stated, "Every ELL student is different. I see that some kids try to find their... own way. They find little subgroups within the school to put themselves." Furthermore, P5 noticed, "Sometimes, they are coping in a way that negatively impacts the class. They are playing around because they're struggling. I've also seen coping in a positive way... they are... able to pair up with others...in the classroom who speak their language." In addition to P4 and P5, P7 stated, "They cope positively. Some days are better than other days. But they usually have positive interactions and positive experiences. They're excited."

In addition, P5 and P6 described similar experiences regarding how ELLs cope within the cultural classroom learning environment. P6 stated,

> "I've witnessed... some students come here...scared. They feel very isolated and left out. Some of them are scared, worried, and don't want to come probably. But I think it affects each of them differently. I do notice they stick together. So, a lot of times I think that helps them. At least they feel more comfortable having a friend. Some of them get excited... to come to school."

P8 expressed the acculturation experiences faced by ELLs as "A culture shock. They don't feel comfortable in the environment. They don't feel safe." She stated, "It's very crucial for ELL students to feel comfortable and be a part of the classroom." However, most of the participants described that ELLs looked for supportive friends who shared similar experiences. For instance, P1, P2, P3, P4, P5, and P6 stated that peer support is crucial to helping ELLs cope within a cultural classroom environment. P1 highlighted that "ELLs interacted with other students in the classroom." She stated that it "depends on where the students come from... home culture environment, they may think that the American school environment is more relaxed." Also, P3 indicated that,

"Everyone's coping differently based on their home life and their past experiences. But some students kind of shut down and withdraw. They are... feeling left out or behind. Other students can overcome those acculturation experiences because they look to their friends for support."

P2 noticed that,

"They tend to find one or two people[*classmates*] that they trust... have similar experiences that help them to get through it as they know that they're not alone. Some of them cope differently. Some adjust fine within... seek friendships with others in the classroom. Some of them cry, but eventually, they get it together."

The study participants described different ways that ELLs coped within the classroom learning environment. For instance, the participants indicated that most ELLs looked for support from their classmates who shared similar experiences with them. The next section discusses Research Question 2.

### *Research Question 2. What Are Teachers' Lived Experiences Addressing the Acculturation of ELLs within the Classroom Learning Environment in the United States?*

Research Question 2 aimed to explore the teachers' experiences of addressing the acculturation experiences of ELLs in the classroom learning environment in the United States. Research Question 2 included three interview questions and three following questions. These interview questions were used to gain meaningful descriptions of the lived experiences of ELLs from teachers' perspectives. The researcher used Giorgi's (2009) five-step data analysis process. Two constituents emerged in response to Research Question 2. Table 3 highlights the constituents.

| Constituent | Total of participants |
| --- | --- |
| 1. Providing culturally relevant classroom learning environment | 8 |
| 2. Lack of teachers' awareness and classroom support | 8 |

*Table 3*. Constituents Describing Teachers' Experiences Addressing the Acculturation of ELLs

### Constituent 1. Providing a Culturally Relevant Classroom Learning Environment.

All study participants described that one of the roles of teachers is to provide a cultural classroom learning environment that supports ELL learning experiences. The constituent provides meaningful descriptions of how teachers address and promote successful acculturation experiences in the United States. P2 revealed the importance of the classroom environment. She stated,

"So, one thing I like to do in the beginning is to set up the classroom. The classroom culture environment is safe for everyone... be accepted. So, setting that foundation from the beginning is huge. I have a couple of new kids that join our classroom. I let them know that this is a safe class and we're here to support and help... along the way as they adjust to the new culture. They're learning how they can use what they've learned from their own culture and how they can incorporate it into the classroom."

P3 also indicated that some ELLs need nonverbal support in the classroom. For instance, P3 stated,

"So, providing reassurance is the most important tool that I use for addressing these experiences. I want the students to know that just because they're not comfortable with English yet... that does not mean they can't be successful. If the students are very limited in English, I try to use nonverbal cues, like giving them a thumbs-up or a thumbs-down or just smiling."

Unlike P2 and P3, who shared their concerns about creating a suitable environment for their ELLs to acclimate to the new cultural learning experiences, P4 indicated, "I feel like our hands are tied a little bit because you do not have the resources or the schedule is not permitted." On the other hand, P5 shared, "One thing I… do is I learn keywords and key phrases in their language so I can better assist. Introduce vocabulary words; I utilize different cognates… pictures… and classmate who speaks their language to help."

P1, P7, and P8 explained the role of the teacher is to be patient and assist ELLs. For instance, P7 noted that "I model the English language. I speak the language and repeat it." Also, she expressed the need to "Build a positive relationship with them immediately. You're safe. You're okay. Everything is going to be okay. We're in a classroom where we're all friends." Similarly, P8 indicated, "With the repetitiveness of the same words repeatedly, they excel. They jump from one to… three points. They could achieve; they move higher than any other students." P1 expressed that "The main thing is teaching the students to follow the rules and procedures and involve their family in the educational system."

The constituent provides the ways teachers address the acculturation experiences of ELLs by encouraging and maintaining an environment that supports their ELLs as they acclimate to the new cultural setting of the United States. The following constituent describes teachers' challenges in addressing ELLs' acculturation experiences.

**Constituent 2. Lack of Teachers' Awareness and Classroom Support.** All participants of the study expressed the challenges they face in addressing the acculturation experiences of ELLs. For instance, P4 stated,

> "I think there are multiple challenges. I think time is one. I have no available resources or personnel. I don't know how to communicate… with them. I use Google Translate to make them feel welcome, such as hello, Hola, Como Estas, and Bonjour. If the parents help the kids… the students will assimilate within the school. Because if all of their needs are not met, not just food, water, and clothes but all the other social needs."

Also, P5 indicated,

"Many teachers lack knowledge. I have up to 24 kids or even more in your classroom. Everything is all about data. If your data is not looking good, it can be a concern. What happens is that teachers tend to spend less time with our ELL students and more time with the students that we count for our school grades."

Similar to P4 and P5, P1 shared that "Sometimes teachers have a diverse group of students. So it's hard for them [*Teachers*] to know something about every culture. It takes time." Also, P1 used the Google app to communicate with the families… and to guide the students through the process… in the school environment. In addition, P2 and P5 shared similarities regarding the challenges teachers face within the classroom. For instance, P2 noted, "I feel like some teachers may not be aware and may not understand it [*ELLs*]. So that's why they cannot provide the correct support for these students in the classroom. They do not have training."

On the other hand, P3 was concerned about the classroom's procedures. For instance, P3 stated, "I would say that one of the challenges I face is… to convey to them to follow classroom procedures." Also, P6 stated, "I'm trying to teach them; it's hard. They're still nervous or scared." Like P6, P7 suggested, "Differentiating the instructions… to meet their needs and try to help them connecting, using visuals… classmates, and using technology." However, P8 expressed that one of the ways to address the challenges of teaching ELLs is that "The kids are very good with technology… pulling their culture into the classroom and making them feel a part of the curriculum."

The participants of the study expressed that addressing the challenges faced by ELLs required resources and knowledge of the acculturation experiences of ELLs. Some ways they shared include technology, pictures, professional training for teachers, and peer support from the other students and school staff. The following section discusses Research Question 3.

***Research Question 3. What Are the Strategies That Teachers Use to***

***Address the Acculturation Experiences of ELLs Within the Classroom
Learning Environments in the United States?***

This research question aimed to explore the strategies teachers use to
address the acculturation experiences of ELLs within the classroom
learning environment in the United States. Through several interview
questions, the study participants described strategies they used to address
the acculturation of ELLs. The participant's interview transcripts
revealed two constituents related to the acculturation experiences of
ELLs. Table 4 highlights the constituents.

| Constituent | Total of participants |
|---|---|
| 1. Native language support and visual classroom presentations | 8 |
| 2. Creating a culturally inclusive classroom environment | 8 |
| 3. Culturally classroom resources and bilingual support to help ELLs | 8 |

*Table 4.* Constituents Describing Strategies for Addressing the Acculturation
Experiences of ELLs

**Constituent 1. Native Language Support and Visual Classroom
Presentations.** The study participants shared strategies they used to
support ELLs' acculturation experiences within the classroom learning
environment. The participants described using native language support
and visual resources to help ELLs assimilate into their classroom environment when they first arrived in the United States and the school
setting. P2 described,

"So, I translate a lot of their native language.

I try to provide the academic vocabulary words in their native
language. So, if I'm going over a couple of words... I show them a
picture, image, and vocabulary words so they can understand... I tend to
support them in their home language if they speak Creole. They feel
more comfortable... because I know their culture. I use Google Translate
for my Spanish speakers... so they don't feel lost."

P3 also shared the importance of using and providing meaningful support to ELLs while assimilating into the new learning environment. She stated,

"So, I would say the first thing that I do is... I organize my classroom. I try to label the most commonly used things in my classroom, like the board, the instruments, and the bathroom. I have them in English, Spanish, and Creole... that way, they build vocabulary. I also have assigned seating... which allows me to pair the students with other students who speak their first language. I try to create an environment where students can still be proud of their culture... feel represented by their culture, and assimilate to educational norms in the classroom. That doesn't always mean that the students have to erase their cultural identity in that process entirely."

P5, P3, P6, and P7 also used cultural and visual supports to create a suitable classroom learning environment for their ELLs. For example, P5 indicated, "I use pictures in the classroom and have their flag represented. I have a bulletin board with the different things." In addition, P6 noted that "I've definitely used cultural support and other students translate. I have asked them about their home life. One little boy loves to tell me about Haiti and everything about it. He always makes the connection back to Haiti." Furthermore, P7 shared that "Building that trust, getting to know families... I use a lot of visuals and pictures and try to use vocabulary words with pictures so they can see... It helps them make connections." Like P7, P4 believed that knowing and understanding the ELLs' background is essential. P4 stated, "I try to ask the kids about their experience and how they got here. I always get stories, and I like to hear them."

Like P6, P1 used the student's prior experiences, such as their cultural experience. She stated,

"Of course, we honor the students' culture. We recognize the student's culture. We include it in our lessons or school-wide activities. We develop an asset point of view, not a deficit point of view. It means that we value the student's cultural background. If the ELLs can maintain their home culture and acculturate to the American culture, they become bicultural. That can give them a more positive learning experience, leading to their success... and achievements."

The participants emphasized the importance of providing and maintaining the appropriate classroom learning experiences for ELLs to assimilate into the United States's classroom culture.

**Constituent 2. Creating a Culturally Inclusive Classroom Environment.** All study participants presented and shared similar descriptions regarding the assimilation experiences of ELLs within the classroom learning environment.

First of all, P1 stated,

"I like to try to build relationships with all my ELLs. I want them to feel confident and successful. It does affect their motivations positively. I think generally they are successful. They are academically successful. They understand why they're in school so they can live a better life because, in most cases… immigrants come to America; after all, they want a better life for themselves and their children."

Also, P3 noticed similar experiences that ELLs displayed during the acculturation process. She indicated,

"Verbal encouragement to let them know that it's okay. I understand you, and that's why I'm here to help you. They usually respond positively when they overcome those experiences. They realize that they can still maintain their identity and culture while learning the new social norms of the new culture. They're more likely to reach out and try new things, make new friends, and… do things that scare them. Once they start seeing those doors opening up for them, they're more likely to overcome their barriers."

In addition, P5, P6, P7, and P8 shared similar descriptions of ELLs assimilation experiences within the classroom learning environment. P5 noted,

"They may leap for joy with smiles on their face. They're just happy, and then they're ready to go on to the next challenge. They're prepared to take on more because it's in the celebration of the small victories that they're confident. Their confidence is built up, and resiliency is part of that as well. So, they're learning how to push through and not just push through for this moment, but it's one of those traits needed for life. And so, it's very awesome to see."

For instance, P6 stated,

"I always give them verbal encouragement to let them know that it is okay and that I understand, and that is why I'm here to try to help them learn the language. Understanding their culture, having a classroom where you are motivating, ensuring the environment is conducive to learning and genuine care, and creating a safe space. I think they're relieved and happy. They love that success. Even if it's… one point up to me for them, that's the world. Next time, we go for two points. We keep moving forward. They definitely can learn; they will know it. Just keep telling them… okay, you will get there."

Like P6, P7 indicated,

"They're pleased with their confidence. They're excited. You could see it in their face. You can see it in their behavior. Then, they start participating and yelling out answers to the other kids. When they get it, that light goes on! That's what they're doing, and they are showing it. They passed something on the technology. It tells them whether they passed, and it gives them a score. I got a hundred, so they shared, and that's exciting."

Furthermore, P4, P2, and P8 described some successful experiences of ELLs. For instance, P4 mentioned,

"The first six months were a little bit rocky for them. But after that, they flourish in every way. Socially, they have made friends… they are communicated. They have read books. I'm so proud because of that intrinsic motivation; they thrive no matter where they are."

Like P4, P2 stated that "They're excited. It makes them want to grow and learn. You see them more involved in the classroom. You see that the relationships… they start making with the other kids are more positive." Also, P8 indicated, "ELLs respond successfully because they do not want to let the teacher down. They do successful work."

**Constituent 3. Culturally Classroom Resources and Bilingual**

**Support to Help ELLs.** The study participants described the challenges ELLs faced within the classroom learning environment and teachers' challenges in providing relevant classroom support to ELLs. The participants described some successful acculturation experiences of ELLs within the classroom learning environment. (In addition, participants suggested some meaningful strategies to meet the needs of ELLs in the United States. For instance, P1 stated, "I think we can always ask for resources. We can check in with teammates with the same...cultural experiences." Also, P2 stated,

"ELLs need to have more teachers who understand them and more people on the campus who speak their native language to help them... provide more lessons in dual language... and support them in their native language so they can adjust well to this new environment. Also, breaking down the lessons and making them [*Lessons*] more understandable for the students. Provide visuals for the students and the difficult words or vocabulary words in their native language... resources that support them in adjusting... and understanding in some ways."

P4 also indicated that "I said... a few phrases in different languages. I used Google Translate to communicate with the students. I tried to understand and figure out how they were feeling." In addition, P5 stated, "To meet their needs, I would say that as a teacher, I must make sure they feel loved in the classroom. So, once I have met that need, I can move on to their academics and the different needs that they have." P3 said, "The first thing is always allowing students to express concerns. If they have something that they want to bring up... always be open-minded to it. I try to make them feel extremely comfortable in my classroom... and maintain a safe environment."

In addition, P6, P7, and P8 shared some meaningful descriptions regarding meeting the needs of ELLs. For instance, P6 stated, "I use someone who speaks their language... because I do not have many resources. We have dictionaries, cognates... and pictures... anything that helps." Furthermore, P7 noted, "I ask many questions, allowing interaction with other kids, establishing a welcoming, friendly relationship with them. I want to say that parent support is critical in helping and teaching ELLs…in the classroom." Also, P8 stated,

> "There are a variety of different ways. It depends on where they are. So, I have cultural books for those ELL students in the classroom to make them feel a part of the lessons."

All participants described meeting the needs of ELLs within the classroom learning environment as part of their classroom strategies. Participants created a classroom environment that is safe and welcoming for ELLs. For instance, participants expressed that classmates who speak the same language and have the same cultural background are beneficial resources to meet the needs of ELLs. Also, participants stated that parental involvement and resources in the native language are vital factors in meeting these kids' needs. Some other elements that participants described included technology and visual resources in teaching and making the learning experiences more culturable for ELLs. The following section discusses the evaluation of the findings.

## Evaluation of the Findings

The evaluation of the findings focused on the three research questions and the study's theoretical framework. The theoretical framework of this study is Berry's (1997) acculturation theory. Acculturation theories have been used to explain the cultural changes immigrants face during acculturation. Some of the contributors to acculturation theories include Gordon (1964), Redfield et al. (1936), and Schumann (1978). Berry's (1997) acculturation theory is focused on the lived experiences of immigrants and their acculturation experiences in the host culture. Berry's (1997) acculturation theory has been used to investigate the cultural changes of immigrants and refugees in adaptation to North American, Australian, European, Asian, African, and South American settings. Berry's (1997) acculturation theory provides four strategies to explain the acculturation process of immigrants. Berry's (1997) acculturation strategies are assimilation, separation, integration, and marginalization.

The meaningful constituents emerged through data collected in response to the research questions of this study. These constituents are consistent with the current literature review and Berry's (1997) acculturation theory that guided this study. The following section evaluates each finding through the lens of literature and the study's theoretical framework.

### *Research Question 1. What Are Teachers' Lived Experiences of the Acculturation Faced by ELLs within the Classroom Learning Environment in the United States?*

**Constituent 1. ELLs Disconnected from the Classroom.** According to the existing research, this constituent was not a surprise. This constituent described ELLs as disconnected from the classroom, becoming more reserved about participating in classroom activities and facing challenges adapting to the new learning environment. Also, ELLs have a hard time acclimating within the classroom learning environment. For instance, ELLs are often very quiet, lost, fearful, scared, and confused. The current studies found that ELLs struggle to integrate and assimilate into the new cultural classroom environments (Khoo & Kang, 2022; Schneider & Kulmhofer-Bommer, 2022; Watkinson et al., 2022; Wei, 2021). According to Parker et al. (2021), ELLs have experienced social isolation and loneliness. Also, this constituent was consistent with Stark et al.'s (2021) findings. According to Stark et al. (2021), ELLs are separated and experience embarrassment, frustration, and anxiety as they acclimate to the new environment.

Berry's (1997) acculturation theory explains this constituent through its separation strategy. The separation strategy is one of the four strategies of Berry's (1997) acculturation theory. According to the separation strategy, this constituent can be understood as individuals who oppose the host culture; often, they are afraid to explore the new culture and disconnect from the primary culture (Berry, 1997). The significance of this constituent as it relates to acculturation theory also provides an understanding of the acculturation experiences of ELLs within the classroom learning environment. Furthermore, this constituent can be understood as the result of ELLs opposed to acculturation experiences. Also, they are disconnected and experience more depression, anxiety, and acculturation stress in assimilating to new environments (Berry & Hou, 2016). Therefore, this constituent can be understood as isolated, lonely, fearful, and confused experiences that ELLs encounter within the classroom learning environment (Berry, 1997).

**Constituent 2. English Language Barriers Faced by ELLs.** This constituent described the English language barriers of ELLs. This constituent revealed that English language barriers were one of the most significant challenges faced by ELLs when they arrived in the United States. Also, ELLs have to learn the English language, and often, they do not understand what is happening in the classroom. For instance, ELLs do not know enough vocabulary words to make this transition more accessible for communicating with their classmates and others. Therefore, this finding was not a surprise. According to Kennedy and McLoughlin (2023), ELLs struggle with all kinds of English language skills, such as reading, writing, listening, and speaking. For instance, the researchers found that ELLs struggle to communicate due to limited English language skills and an inability to express their ideas, understand work materials, and engage in classroom interactions (Dewi et al., 2021; Hsin et al., 2022).

According to Berry's (1997) acculturation theory, the constituent, English language barriers faced by ELLs, can be understood as acculturation stress experiences faced by ELLs within the classroom learning environment. This constituent relates to social isolation, academic pressure, and insufficiency in English language background that ELLs encounter to assimilate into the new classroom culture. Also, this constituent can be understood through the lens of acculturation theory. According to Berry and Hou's (2016) study, there was significant evidence that the separation strategy has dramatically impacted the lived experiences of immigrants while adapting to the host culture environment and its components. According to Berry's (1997) acculturation theory, a separation strategy—this constituent—can be understood as individuals who oppose the host culture and are reluctant to explore the new culture and remain in their own culture. Therefore, this constituent can be understood as the lack of interest and multiple challenges ELLs face to acclimate to the new learning environment, learn the English language, and develop a sense of belonging (Berry & Hou, 2016).

**Constituent 3. Academic Disadvantages Faced by ELLs Within**

**the Classroom**. This constituent addressed the academic disadvantages faced by ELLs. However, this constituent was not surprised. For instance, ELLs struggle academically due to acculturation experiences and lack of academic support, prior schooling, family support, and class-room support. However, current studies found that ELLs' academic achievement is significantly lower than other groups of students (Owens & Wells, 2021). According to Zhang et al. (2022), ELLs lack English language skills, which are vital for them to be successful academically, socially, and culturally (Zhang et al., 2022). Also, ELLs endure linguistic challenges that impact their academic achievement (Zhang et al., 2022). The academic achievements of ELLs are problematic and alarming compared to non-ELL students (Huang, 2022; Zhang et al., 2022).

In addition, the constituent can be understood in light of the integration strategy, which is one of the components of Berry's (1997) accultur-ation theory that explored the lived experiences of individuals. According to Berry (1997), individuals who adopted the integration strategy experienced more academic success and social interactions than immigrants who adopted the separation strategy. Therefore, the constituent can be understood through the lens of integration and separa-tion strategies, two opposing components of Berry's (1997) acculturation theory. According to Berry's (1997) acculturation theory, the integration strategy provides supportive evidence that individuals are more successful when they keep a positive attitude toward the host culture and their primary culture, both socially and academically. Also, this constituent can be understood through the lens of separation strategy as it relates to academic disadvantages faced by ELLs within the classroom because they are afraid to explore the new school culture, as opposed to new cultural experiences, and prefer to stay in their own society (Berry, 1997; Berry & Hou, 2016).


**Constituent 4. The Challenges Faced by ELLs to Cope Within the Classroom.** The constituent defined the challenges ELLs face in coping with the classroom environment. For instance, some ELLs were isolated, scared, and worried and experienced culture shock in the classroom learning environment. This constituent was not surprised. According to the studies by Gilblom et al. (2022), Fang (2020), and Stark et al. (2021), acculturation experiences are often associated with social isolation and loneliness. Furthermore, The acculturation experiences faced by ELLs contributed to the difficulties integrating into the school culture environment (Khoo & Kang, 2022; Schneider & Kulmhofer-Bommer, 2022; Watkinson et al., 2022; Wei, 2021).

According to Berry's (1997) acculturation theory, the constituent can be understood through the lens of the separation strategy, which indicates that individuals are afraid to explore a new culture and prefer to stay in their own society. According to Berry and Hou (2016), individuals are often afraid to acclimate to a new school culture, stay in their group, and lack interest in experiencing the new cultural environment. Furthermore, this constituent can be understood as it relates to the resistance and rejection many ELLs have encountered within the classroom learning environment. According to acculturation theory, it is the most negative experience and consequence of the immigrants' effort to join the new cultural environment because they lack the sense of belonging, acceptance, and security to assimilate to the new environment (Berry & Hou, 2016). Research Question 2 is addressed in the next section.

### Research Question 2. What Are Teachers' Lived Experiences Addressing the Acculturation of ELLs Within the Classroom Learning Environment in the United States?

**Constituent 1. Providing Culturally Relevant Classroom Learning Environment.** The constituent addressed the classroom environment. The constituent revealed that one of the roles of teachers is to set a classroom cultural environment that is safe and accepted by everyone. Setting the classroom environment initially provides reassurance and comfort for ELLs to succeed. The constituent was not surprised. For instance, ELLs enjoy their learning process in a conducive environment when they feel that their teachers demonstrate perceptions, promoting self-confidence and academic goals (Adams & Hord, 2023). Also, Irby et al. (2020) stated that teachers have set expectations and perceptions concerning the needs of ELLs. Cho et al. (2020) explored factors that influence ELLs' cultural and linguistic needs. The researchers found that ELLs become more involved and willing to take risks when teachers create an enjoyable atmosphere in the classroom environments (Cho et al., 2020).

According to Berry and Hou's (2016) study, acculturation theory can explain the constituent. Berry and Hou (2016) explored immigrants' sense of belonging while transitioning into the new society and cultural changes. The sense of belonging occurs when the immigrants feel accepted, secure, and adapted to the host country (Berry & Hou, 2016). Also, the constituent can be understood through assimilation and integration strategies, the two essential components of Berry's (1997) acculturation theory. According to Berry's (1997) and Berry and Hou's (2016) studies, these acculturative strategies are relevant to providing a cultural classroom learning environment that promotes the acculturation experiences of ELLs and immigrants toward the larger society and the host culture. Also, the constituent, providing a cultural classroom learning environment, is associated with less acculturative stress and negative experiences for ELLs within the classroom learning environment. In addition, the constituent can be understood as cultural support that ELLs need to integrate into their new learning environment successfully, and it relates to the importance of creating a more welcoming atmosphere, believing that ELLs can reach their dreams as students (Adams & Hord, 2023).

**Constituent 2. Lack of Teachers' Awareness and Classroom Support.** The constituent addressed teachers' awareness of the acculturation of ELLs. For instance, some teachers lack cultural background awareness, resources, limited time, and language barriers to support ELLs in the classroom. It is hard to communicate with ELLs, which is frustrating and nervous for the teachers and their students. The constituent was not surprised. According to Li and Jee (2021), teachers must acknowledge and be aware of the challenges of teaching ELLs and understand their needs. Furthermore, Al-Krenawi et al. (2021) examined the acculturative stress of immigrants enrolled in United States schools. The lack of cultural understanding, mistrust, and psychological stress have impacted the classroom learning experiences (Al-Krenawi et al., 2021).

According to Berry's (1997) acculturation theory, the constituent can further understand the lived experiences of ELLs within the classroom learning environment with their teachers through the component of integration. Berry and Hou (2016) used acculturation theory to explore immigrants' sense of belonging during their transition into the new society and culture changes. The sense of belonging occurs when the immigrants feel accepted, secure, and adapted to the host country (Berry & Hou, 2016). Berry and Hou (2016) showed that the integration strategy was the most preferred among Berry's acculturation strategies. Also, the study's results indicated that social factors influence immigrants who attach to their heritage culture and engage with the host culture to achieve a greater sense of well-being (Berry & Hou, 2016). Also, the constituent can be understood considering that teachers' awareness is essential for supporting all ELLs in assimilating to the new cultural setting and creating a classroom environment that promotes a sense of belonging for all students. Research question three is discussed in the next section of the study.

### *Research Question 3. What Are the Strategies That Teachers Use to Address the Acculturation Experiences of ELLs Within the Classroom Learning Environments in the United States?*

**Constituent 1. Native Language Support and Visual Classroom Presentations.** This constituent described the native language of ELLs and provided academic vocabulary words in their native language. In addition, teachers utilized images in their home language, paired ELLs with other students who speak their first language, built up trust, and utilized their cultural background experiences. The constituent was not surprised. For instance, the existing studies revealed that ELLs learn more effectively when the classroom environment is culturally safe, relevant, and supported by the teachers (Cho et al., 2019; Hong et al., 2019).

According to Adams and Hord (2023), ELLs enjoy a conducive class-room learning environment that is culturally relevant to their learning experiences.

This constituent, native language support and visual classroom presentations can be understood through the lens of the integration strategy, which is one of the components of Berry's (1997) acculturation theory. According to Berry and Hou (2016), integration is associated with acculturative and learning strategies that promote and encourage immigrants to value their previous experiences and heritage culture and engage in the new cultural learning environment to achieve a greater sense of well-being. Therefore, the constituent can be understood by teachers providing cultural stories and opportunities for ELLs to integrate their prior knowledge, including native language literacy skills, where ELLs can be more comfortable and confident in taking risks to explore the new cultural learning environment because they feel safe, supported, and celebrated by their teachers (Berry & Hou, 2016; Maarouf, 2019).

**Constituent 2. Creating a Culturally Inclusive Classroom Environment.** The constituent described ELLs' successful assimilation experiences within the classroom. Some ELLs flourished socially and academically. They communicated with others and participated positively in the classroom activities. They celebrated the small victories and became more confident about themselves. The constituent was not surprised. For instance, Cho et al. (2020) revealed that ELLs become more involved and willing to take risks when teachers create an enjoyable atmosphere by making classroom environments appropriate and safe. According to Owens and Wells (2021), building a culturally appropriate learning environment and a welcoming learning atmosphere increases ELLs' positive experiences and academic achievement. Liaqat et al. (2021) stated that ELLs tend to integrate, assimilate, and engage in the new cultural learning environment when they receive social and cultural support from other individuals.

According to Berry (1997), the constituent can be understood by considering the acculturation theory to investigate the cultural changes of immigrants and refugees in adaptation to the new environment. More specifically, the constituent of creating a culturally inclusive classroom environment can be understood through the lens of the integration strategy, which is one of the widely used and successful components of Berry's (1997) acculturation theory regarding the acculturation experiences of immigrants, including ELLs. According to Berry and Hou (2016), integration is associated with acculturative strategies and learning strategies that support individuals in valuing their previous experiences and heritage culture experiences and engaging in the new cultural learning environment to achieve greater well-being. Therefore, a culturally inclusive environment is essential for supporting students in assimilating to the new cultural educational setting (Berry & Hou, 2016; Guo et al., 2020).

**Constituent 3. Culturally Classroom Resources and Bilingual Support to Help ELL.** The constituent addressed how to meet the needs of ELLs in the United States. The constituent described that teachers need more resources to support ELLs effectively. Some suggestions to meet the needs of ELLs include breaking down the lessons and making the lessons more understandable for ELLs. Also, ELLs learn more effectively when the teachers use visual organizers, maintain a safe cultural classroom learning environment, and provide culturally relevant resources and support. The constituent was not surprised. The current research stated that building a culturally appropriate learning environment and a welcoming learning atmosphere increases the academic achievement of ELLs (Owens & Wells, 2021). The findings of this study aligned with Gilblom et al.'s (2022) study. The researchers found that a culturally inclusion classroom environment is critical for the acculturation experiences of ELLs (Gilblom et al., 2022).

The constituent can be understood through acculturation theory. According to Berry's (1997) acculturation theory, the integration strategy provides the most applicable acculturation avenues that support immigrants' lived experiences in acclimating to the new learning environment. In addition, the constituent can be understood through the integration strategy because it relates to the need to integrate minority group cultures and resources into a larger society, which is an essential aspect of the acculturation process of the population of ELLs. There is a need for more culturally and linguistically equitable classroom resources and opportunities for ELLs (Montgomery et al., 2021). The next session discussed the chapter summary.

## Summary

The problem addressed by this study was the acculturation experiences of ELLs within the classroom learning environment in the United States (Bennouna et al., 2021; Hendy & Cuevas, 2020; Hong et al., 2019; Murray, 2020; Soland & Sandilos, 2021). This qualitative, descriptive phenomenological study aimed to explore the acculturation experiences of ELLs within the classroom learning environment in the United States. Giorgi's (2009) descriptive phenomenological design was used through semi-structured interviews to describe the acculturation experiences of ELLs within the classroom learning environment in the United States. Giorgi's (2009) research design was the essential approach to understanding the essence of the lived experiences faced by ELLs within the classroom learning environment. Purposive sampling was used to recruit the participants based on the study criteria. Pseudonyms were used to protect the identities of the participants. Therefore, P1-P8 represented the participants of the study. Berry's (1997) acculturation theory was used to describe the acculturation experiences of ELLs within the classroom learning environment. Giorgi's (2009) five-step data analysis approach was used to analyze the study's data. Nine meaningful constituents emerged from the study.

The study described the acculturation experiences of ELLs within the classroom learning environment in the United States. The study's findings revealed that ELLs are students whose primary language is not English. ELLs often have different cultural backgrounds and come from several countries. Participants indicated that upon the ELLs' arrival in the classroom learning environment, ELLs face several challenges to acculturation in the new educational settings. Often, ELLs tend to be quiet. ELLs struggle academically due to the English language barrier. Therefore, the participants described that teachers need more classroom resources and appropriate support to meet the needs of all ELLs. However, the participants shared that ELLs assimilated and made more academic progress when the teachers created and provided a classroom learning environment that promotes and accepts diverse cultural backgrounds. Chapter Five discusses the implications, future research recommendations, and the study's conclusions.

The problem addressed by this study was the acculturation experiences of ELLs within the classroom learning environment in the United States (Bennouna et al., 2021; Hendy & Cuevas, 2020; Hong et al., 2019; Murray, 2020; Soland & Sandilos, 2021). The population of ELLs is the fastest-growing group of students in the United States across educational settings (Gilblom et al., 2022; Shim & Shur, 2018; Watkinson et al., 2022). The population of ELLs in the United States has increased since the last decade (Zhang et al., 2022) and has become more diverse (Johnson & Thorne-Wallington, 2021). The researchers indicated that by 2025, one in four students in the United States will be an ELL (Shim & Shur, 2018). However, ELLs have faced tremendous challenges in acclimating to the new learning environment (Ma & Xia, 2021; Watkinson et al., 2022). The challenges faced by ELLs include the acculturation experiences of assimilating to the new school culture environment, challenges in learning the English language, and lower academic achievement (Stark et al., 2021; Watkinson et al., 2022). Researchers described that some of the acculturation experiences ELLs faced within the classroom learning manifested as worry, fear, embarrassment, frustration, and anxiety (Parker et al., 2021). These acculturation experiences increase the stress on ELLs as they try to integrate into the new classroom cultural learning environment (Gilblom et al., 2022; Parker et al., 2021).

The purpose of this qualitative, descriptive phenomenological study was to explore the acculturation experiences of ELLs within the classroom learning environment in the United States. A qualitative method was a unique avenue to explore the lived experiences of the phenomenon of ELLs (Creswell, 2013, 2014). A qualitative method was used to describe the acculturation experiences of ELLs within the classroom learning environment. A qualitative method is appropriate for exploring human phenomena (Creswell & Cage, 2019). Also, a qualitative method is the primary approach to truthfully and succinctly providing the experiences of individuals in a natural setting (Creswell & Cage, 2019).

The appropriate design selected for this study was Amedeo Giorgi's (2009) descriptive phenomenological design. Giorgi's (2009) descriptive phenomenological design was the essential approach to describe the acculturation of lived experiences of ELLs. The research questions were developed. Also, the interview questions were developed and reviewed by a panel of three experts to ensure that the questions were suitable for exploring the phenomenon of the study. This study used interviews to explore the phenomenon. An interview is a communication between the researcher and the study participants (Kvale, 1996). This form of conversation has been applied in qualitative studies to explore human phenomena (Kvale, 1996). According to Kvale (1996), interviews are essential for obtaining an individual's real-life experience. The data were collected through semi-structured interviews. The participants were one male and seven female certified elementary teachers in the Southeastern United States. Therefore, Giorgi's (2009) five-step data analysis process was used to describe the acculturation experiences of ELLs within the classroom learning environment.

Nine meaningful constituents emerged in response to three research questions. Four constituents were identified in response to research question one. The constituents were ELLs disconnected from the classroom, English language barriers faced by ELLs, academic disadvantages faced by ELLs within the classroom, and the challenges faced by ELLs to cope within the classroom. Also, two constituents emerged in response to research question two. The constituents were providing a culturally relevant classroom learning environment, but there was a lack of teachers' awareness and classroom support. In response to Research Question 3, another three meaningful constituents emerged. The constituents were native language support and visual classroom presentations, creating a culturally inclusive classroom environment, and cultural classroom resources and bilingual support to help ELLs.

Furthermore, this study met trustworthiness criteria, which included credibility, dependability, confirmability, and transferability (Lincoln & Guba, 1986). The trustworthiness of a qualitative study depends on the process of collecting the data and the careful interpretation of the data to ensure the quality of the study (Guba, 1981). Also, this study included several limitations. Limitations are factors over which the researcher has no control (Theofanidis & Fountouki, 2018). The first limitation was self-reported data, which included the demographic questionnaire and semi-structured interviews. The study used a member-checking process to improve its trustworthiness. To mitigate this limitation, the researcher created an appropriate environment and believed that the participants' descriptions of the acculturation experiences of ELLs in the classroom were meaningful.

The second limitation of the study was that this qualitative study aimed to explore ELLs' acculturation experiences through teachers who have experience working with ELLs. Therefore, the findings were limited to that population. To mitigate this limitation, inclusion and exclusion criteria were used to recruit the study participants. The third limitation of the study was the demographic and geographical location. The ELL population included students from diverse cultural backgrounds. The study participants may not have direct experiences with all students who compose the population of ELLs. The participants may lack cultural awareness to describe the relevant challenges faced by ELLs. Therefore, the participants' descriptions of the phenomenon may not be consistent with other groups of ELLs due to the socioeconomic, sociocultural, and geographical components of the ELL population. To mitigate this limitation, the researcher increased the study's sample size and recruited eight participants from different cultural backgrounds in the Southeastern United States. I completed all the CITI training. Also, IRB approval was granted from NU, and site authorization and permission were obtained from the school district and an elementary school. Finally, informed consent was provided to the participants with details about the study.

## Implications

The findings of this descriptive phenomenological study were consistent with the literature review and supported the descriptions and efforts to understand the acculturation experiences faced by ELLs within the classroom learning environment through three research questions.

Research Question 1 addressed teachers' experiences of the acculturation ELLs face in the classroom. Research Question 2 described teachers' experiences addressing the acculturation of ELLs within the classroom. Research Question 3 indicated strategies teachers use to address the acculturation experiences of ELLs within the classroom. Through three research questions, nine meaningful constituents emerged from the study.

***Research Question 1. What Are Teachers' Lived Experiences of the Acculturation Faced by ELLs Within the Classroom Learning Environment in the United States?***

**Constituent 1. ELLs Disconnected from the Classroom.** In response to Research Question 1, the findings of this constituent revealed that some ELLs disconnected from their classroom and faced multiple challenges to acculturate into the classroom learning environment. Often, ELLs are reserved and afraid to participate in classroom activities. Also, ELLs are very quiet, a little bit lost, fearful, scared, and confused. The findings of this constituent were consistent with and supported by the current studies. For instance, Andrei and Northrop (2022) found that ELLs constitute the most important group of students in the United States public schools, and approximately 10% of K-12th grade students are ELLs across the nation's schools. Furthermore, Kennedy and McLoughlin (2023) claimed that one in five students in the United States are ELLs because their primary language is not English; they face significant challenges, and their needs are unique due to their cultural and language differences. Also, the findings of this constituent are consistent with Parker et al.'s (2021) study. Researchers have found that isolation and loneliness were among some difficulties the population of ELLs encountered at the beginning of their classroom experiences (Parker et al., 2021). Stark et al. (2021) conducted similar research and found that the acculturation experienced by the ELL population includes embarrassment and frustrations, and such experiences impacted their motivation to assimilate within the classroom learning settings.

The findings of this constituent contribute to and enhance the knowledge of the theoretical framework of the study, Berry's (1997) acculturation theory. Constituent 1, ELLs disconnected from the classroom, provides the most meaningful descriptions of the acculturation experiences of ELLs within the classroom learning environment. The findings of this constituent also align with the separation strategy, which is one of the components of Berry's (1997) acculturation theory. The separation strategy relates to individuals who oppose the host culture and keep their own place; they are usually afraid to explore the new culture, and they prefer to stay in their own society (Berry, 1997; Berry & Hou, 2016). Furthermore, this constituent one, ELLs disconnected from the classroom, contributes and enhances the knowledge that relates to the separation strategy, which indicates that the sense of disengagement occurs when the individuals are opposed to the host culture experiences (Berry & Hou, 2016).

**Constituent 2. English Language Barriers Faced by ELLs.** In response to Research Question 1, the findings of this constituent, English language barriers faced by ELLs, revealed that one of the major barriers faced by the population of ELLs is the English language barrier to acclimating to the new cultural classroom learning environment. For instance, the findings indicated that ELLs do not understand what is going on in the classroom. Often, ELLs lack vocabulary words to express themselves, making this transition easier. The findings of this constituent are reinforced by previous studies. For instance, the researchers stated that ELLs encounter an English language barrier when communicating with others (Dewi et al., 2021). Also, Hsin et al. (2022) found that the English language barrier has impacted ELLs' social-cultural interactions and abilities to express their ideas, understand work materials, and engage in classroom activities. Therefore, the English language barrier becomes a challenge for ELLs to assimilate into the new classroom learning environment (Dewi et al., 2021; Hsin et al., 2022).

The findings of this constituent enhance the knowledge of Berry's (1997) acculturation theory. The significance of research on Berry's (1997) acculturation theory is that it is consistent in understanding the acculturation experiences of individuals who are adapting to a new cultural environment. Also, this constituent relates to the separation strategy, which is one of the components of Berry's (1997) acculturation theory that indicates individuals who oppose the host culture are often afraid to explore the new culture and prefer to stay in their own society. Therefore, individuals who face an English language barrier also encounter more difficulties in experiencing a sense of belonging, acceptance, and security in assimilating into the new environment (Berry & Hou, 2016).

**Constituent 3. Academic Disadvantages Faced by ELLs Within the Classroom.** In response to Research Question 1, the findings of this constituent, academic disadvantages faced by ELLs within the classroom revealed the academic disadvantages faced by ELLs upon arrival in the classroom learning environment in the United States. For instance, the findings revealed that ELLs struggle academically because they are tested in English while they face an English language barrier and challenges to assimilating into cultural classroom learning settings. However, the findings showed that some of the ELLs do well once they feel safe. Also, the findings indicated that the academic achievement of ELLs is associated with previous school experiences, family support, classroom support, and the socioeconomic status of the family, and depends on how long the students have been in the United States. The findings of this constituent relate to the current studies. According to Owens and Wells (2021), the academic achievement of ELLs is significantly lower compared to the academic achievement of non-ELL students. Also, the researchers stated that ELLs lack essential English language skills to be successful academically, socially, and culturally (Zhang et al., 2022). The reading scores for fourth, eighth, and tenth grades among ELLs were inferior and lower compared to their peers (Zhang et al., 2022). For instance, only 1% of ELLs met the English language proficiency level (Zhang et al., 2022).

The findings of this constituent contribute to and enhance the knowledge of Berry's (1997) acculturation theory, more specifically, the integration strategy, which is one of the components of the framework of this study. The significance of this constituent contributes to Berry's (1997) acculturation theory, and it is consistent with understanding the acculturation experiences of ELLs who are adapting to the new cultural environment and doing well academically. According to Berry and Hou (2016), the integration strategy, which is the most preferred strategy, is associated with successful assimilation. Therefore, individuals who engage in applying the integration strategy within the host culture often tend to achieve a greater sense of well-being and become more successful academically (Berry & Hou, 2016). Also, the findings of this constituent enhance the knowledge of Berry's (1997) acculturation theory that suggested that successful acculturation experiences are related to the years, age, and economic status of the immigrants.

**Constituent 4. The Challenges Faced by ELLs to Cope Within the Classroom.** In response to Research Question 1, the findings of this constituent, the challenges faced by ELLs to cope within the classroom demonstrated that ELLs face multiple challenges to cope within the classroom learning environment. For instance, the findings revealed that some ELLs adapt really well by seeking friendships with others in the classroom who speak the language and share the same cultural background upon arrival. However, the findings showed that at the beginning of the acculturation experience, ELLs are very isolated, scared, and worried, and they experience culture shock within the classroom. The findings of this study reinforced previous studies. The researchers revealed that at the beginning of acculturation experiences, ELLs tend to face social isolation, loneliness, embarrassment, and frustration (Fang, 2020). Also, the research showed that the challenges faced by ELLs include socioculturally, low self-motivation, and difficulties integrating into the school culture environment (Khoo & Kang, 2022), manifested as classroom anxiety in the new learning environment (Gilblom et al., 2022).

The findings of this constituent contribute to and enhance the knowledge of Berry's (1997) acculturation theory, more specifically, the integration strategy, which is one of the components of the theoretical framework of this study. Berry (1997) described that immigrants who adopt to the separation strategy often oppose the host culture, are usually afraid to explore the new culture and prefer to stay in their own society.

Therefore, ELLs who are in the separation category lack interest in the host culture and experience less self-motivation to explore acculturation to cope within the classroom settings (Berry, 1997; Ugurel Kamisli, 2021). The next section addresses Research Question 2.

***Research Question 2. What Are Teachers' Lived Experiences Addressing the Acculturation of ELLs Within the Classroom Learning Environment in the United States?***

**Constituent 1. Providing a Culturally Relevant Classroom Learning Environment.** In response to Research Question 2, the findings of this constituent, providing a cultural classroom learning environment, indicated that the first role of a classroom teacher is to set a classroom cultural environment that is safe and accepted by everyone. The findings have shown that setting a conducive classroom environment at the beginning of the acculturation experience provides reassurance and comfort for all ELLs to adapt and acclimate to the new learning environment. The findings of this constituent are consistent with current studies. For instance, the researchers encouraged teachers to create a learning environment that promotes respect for all students (Adams & Hord, 2023). Also, Irby et al. (2020) stated that teachers have a different set of expectations and perceptions with respect to their ELLs compared to mainstream students. Also, Khawaja and Carr's (2020) study revealed that sociocultural support is an important aspect for ELLs to successfully integrate into their new learning environment. Similarly, Liaqat et al.'s (2021) study supported the idea that ELLs tend to integrate, assimilate, and engage in the new cultural learning environment when they receive social and cultural support from other individuals.

The findings of this constituent increase the knowledge of Berry's (1997) acculturation theory, more specifically, the component that relates to the successful acculturation experiences of the immigrants' integration. For instance, Berry and Hou (2016) explored the sense of belonging of immigrants during their transition into the new society and culture changes. The sense of belonging occurs when the immigrants feel accepted and adapted to the host country (Berry & Hou,

2016). The study revealed that immigrants tend to integrate into a new environment when they feel a sense of belonging that is supported and accepted (Berry & Hou, 2016). Therefore, the findings of this constituent, providing a cultural classroom learning environment, contribute to the integration component of Berry's (1997) acculturation theory.

**Constituent 2. Lack of Teachers' Awareness and Classroom Support.** In response to Research Question 2, the findings of this constituent, lack of teachers' awareness and classroom support, revealed several strategies that support the acculturation experiences of ELLs within the classroom learning environment. For instance, some of the strategies honor and recognize the students' cultural backgrounds. The findings of this constituent also indicated that ELLs can maintain their home culture and acculturate to the new culture. However, many teachers lack multicultural awareness to successfully support the ELL population. The findings of this constituent were consistent with the current studies. For instance, Khawaja and Carr (2020) revealed that sociocultural support promotes integration into their new learning environment. Also, Liaqat et al. (2021) stated that ELLs tend to assimilate into the new cultural learning environment when they receive social and cultural support from other individuals.

The findings of this constituent increase the knowledge of Berry's (1997) acculturation theory; more specifically, this constituent relates to assimilation and integration strategies. According to Berry (1997), assimilation is the context in which individuals adopt a positive attitude toward the new culture. Also, assimilation occurs when the individuals receive the host culture (Berry & Hou, 2016) favorably. For instance, the assimilation strategy helps immigrants adapt to the experiences of the new culture (Berry & Hou, 2016). In addition, Berry's (1997) integration strategy promotes the idea that individuals can maintain and value the primary cultural integrity while they become an integral part of the new culture society. Therefore, the findings of this constituent honor and recognize the students' cultural backgrounds, increasing the knowledge of Berry's (1997) acculturation theory that relates to assimilation and integration strategies. Research Question 3 is discussed in the next section of the study.

***Research Question 3. What are the Strategies That Teachers Use to Address the Acculturation Experiences of ELLs within the Classroom Learning Environments in the United States?***

**Constituent 1. Native Language Support and Visual Classroom Presentations.** In response to Research Question 3, the findings of this constituent—native language support and visual classroom presentations—showed the challenges of meeting the needs of ELLs within the classroom. For instance, the lack of resources, limited time, and language barrier to communicate with ELLs and the experiences created frustration and nervousness for everyone. The findings of this constituent indicated the native language of ELLs and provided academic vocabulary words in their native language, utilizing images in their home language, pairing ELLs up with other students who speak their first language, building up trust, and supporting the learner's cultural background experiences. The findings of this constituent were consistent with current studies. For instance, ELLs learn more effectively when the classroom environment is culturally safe, relevant, and supported by the teachers (Cho et al., 2019). According to Adams and Hord (2023), ELLs enjoy a conducive classroom learning environment that is culturally relevant to their prior learning experiences. Also, Li and Jee (2021) expressed the need to address the academic experiences of ELLs within the classroom effectively. Similarly, creating a more welcoming atmosphere is essential for supporting and teaching the population of ELLs (Adams & Hord, 2023).

The findings of this constituent increase the knowledge of Berry's (1997) acculturation theory. For instance, this constituent contributes to understanding the assimilation and integration strategies. According to Berry (1997), the assimilation strategy is a concept that promotes a positive attitude toward the new culture. In addition, Berry's (1997) integration strategy promotes the idea that individuals can maintain and value the primary cultural integrity while becoming an integral part of the new cultural society. Therefore, by creating a classroom atmosphere and providing cultural support, teachers promote ELLs' assimilation and integration experiences within the classroom learning environment.

**Constituent 2. Creating a Culturally Inclusive Classroom Environment.** In response to Research Question 3, the findings of this constituent, creating a culturally inclusive classroom environment, demonstrated that most ELLs are assimilated into the new classroom learning environment. But, in the beginning, the experiences were a little bit "rocky" for some of the ELLs to acclimate to a new cultural classroom learning environment. The findings of this constituent revealed that prior schooling experiences, classroom support, peer support, and parental involvement are essential for the successful acculturation experiences of ELLs. The findings of this study confirmed current studies. For instance, the researchers stated that ELLs suffered from cultural exclusion and experienced cultural disadvantages in their classrooms (Stark et al., 2021). Similarly, Wang and Yu (2021) found that culturally relevant and inclusive classrooms are vital for ELLs to learn the English language effectively and achieve more tremendous academic success.

The findings of this constituent increase the knowledge of Berry's (1997) acculturation theory. For instance, this constituent contributes to understanding the assimilation, integration, separation, and marginalization strategies of Berry's (1997) acculturation theory. For instance, creating a culturally inclusive classroom environment relates to and promotes the assimilation and integration of the individuals within the environment. On the other hand, ELLs who face cultural exclusion and cultural disadvantages in their classroom tend to adopt separation and marginalization strategies (Berry & Hou, 2016). Therefore, the findings of this constituent contribute to the knowledge of all components of Berry's (1997) acculturation theory.

**Constituent 3. Culturally Classroom Resources and Bilingual Support to Help ELLs.** In response to Research Question 3, the findings of this constituent, cultural classroom resources, and bilingual support to help ELLs revealed the classroom strategies to meet the needs of ELLs.

For instance, the findings of this constituent indicated that many teachers feel that they do not have enough resources to effectively support the acculturation experiences of ELLs within the classroom learning environment. The findings of this constituent promote bilingual support for new ELLs, including breaking down the lessons and making the lessons more understandable for them. Also, the findings revealed that ELLs learn more effectively when the teachers use visual resources, maintain a safe cultural classroom learning environment, and provide culturally relevant resources. The findings of the constituent were consistent and confirmed current studies. The researchers stated that building a culturally appropriate learning atmosphere increases the academic achievement of ELLs (Owens & Wells, 2021). Similarly, Montgomery et al. (2021) explored immigrants lived experiences and highlighted the need for more linguistically equitable classroom resources and more opportunities for ELLs to explore the new learning environment (Montgomery et al., 2021). For instance, Castro Olivo et al. (2022) explored a culturally adapted program for ELLs. Researchers found that ELLs often benefit more when the learning environment is appropriate and less stressful (Castro Olivo et al., 2022).

The findings of this constituent increase the knowledge of Berry's (1997) acculturation theory. For instance, this constituent contributes to understanding the four components of Berry's (1997) acculturation theory. According to Berry (1997), cultural communities, cultural maintenance, and the need to integrate minority group cultures into a larger society are essential aspects of the acculturation process for immigrants within the new setting. Therefore, the findings of this constituent honor and recognize the students' cultural backgrounds as resources that enhance and increase the experiences of ELLs as well as the knowledge of Berry's (1997) acculturation theory that relates to successful assimilation and integration.

## Recommendations for Practice

This qualitative, descriptive phenomenological study aimed to explore the acculturation experiences of ELLs within the classroom learning environment in the United States. The study addressed the acculturation experiences of ELLs within the classroom learning environment in the United States (Bennouna et al., 2021, Hendy & Cuevas, 2020; Hong et al., 2019; Murray, 2020; Soland & Sandilos, 2021). The findings of this study shed light on the acculturation experiences of ELLs within the classroom learning environment. The findings of this study indicated that ELLs struggle significantly and become more reserved when acclimating within the classroom learning environment. This study's findings provided several practical recommendations.

The first recommendation is based on Research Question 1 and the findings of Constituent 1, ELLs disconnected from the classroom. The first practical recommendation is that ELLs need more time to acculturate within the classroom and effective culturally relevant classroom support, including peer support, same cultural background, and language experiences. According to Gilblom et al. (2022), cultural inclusion in the classroom environment is critical for the acculturation experiences of ELLs. The findings of this study indicated that it is crucial for ELLs to feel comfortable, feel safe, and become a part of the classroom learning environment.

The second recommendation is based on Research Question 2 and the findings of Constituent 1, providing a cultural classroom learning environment. Teachers must create a culturally relevant classroom environment and promote acceptable classroom diversity that supports effective learning experiences for all students. According to Adams and Hord (2023), one of the roles of a teacher is to develop an atmosphere that promotes classroom integration. In addition, the study's findings revealed that many teachers who lack relevant knowledge regarding ELLs' cultural backgrounds do not have enough bilingual personnel support available in the classroom, lack cultural classroom resources, have limited time, and language barrier between teachers and ELLs.

The third recommendation is based on Research Question 3 and the findings of Constituent 3, cultural classroom resources and bilingual support to help ELLs. Therefore, school districts and school administrators should provide additional resources and professional development for teachers regarding the acculturation experiences of ELLs within the classroom learning environment in the United States. The fact is that ELLs are one of the fastest-growing groups of students in the United States across K-12$^{th}$ grade school settings (Gilblom et al., 2022; Shim & Shur, 2018; Watkinson et al., 2022). Also, the ELL population in the United States has constantly increased (Zhang et al., 2022).

This qualitative, descriptive phenomenological study provided meaningful descriptions of the acculturation experiences of ELLs within the classroom learning environment in the Southeastern United States. Therefore, several recommendations for future practice are suggested to raise awareness of the challenges ELLs face within the classroom learning environment and to provide more strategies to teach ELLs effectively. The findings of this study can lead to new understanding and comprehension that are overdue to help provide culturally relevant classroom support that ELLs desperately need to overcome their challenges and close their academic achievement gaps. This knowledge could promote an effective learning environment for ELLs, provide training opportunities for teachers and school personnel, create culturally inclusive classrooms, provide resources to meet the needs of ELLs, motivate and engage ELLs to assimilate into the English language and help them quickly become part of the new learning environment. The recommendations of this study may be used to advance the body of knowledge relating to ELLs. This qualitative, descriptive phenomenological study provided meaningful descriptions from elementary school teachers' perspectives relevant to ELLs' experiences within the classroom settings. Implementing these recommendations could continue the advancement of practical learning experiences for ELLs and increase their acculturation experiences and academic achievement.

## Recommendations for Future Research

This qualitative descriptive phenomenological study was conducted to describe the acculturation experiences of ELLs within the classroom learning environment in the Southeastern United States. The results and the limitations of the study were presented. Therefore, the following recommendations for future research studies are suggested:

The first recommendation is based on Research Question 1 and the findings of Constituent 1, ELLs disconnected from the classroom. Wang and Yu (2021) argued for a socially, culturally relevant, and inclusive classroom for ELLs in the United States education system. The first recommendation for future research is to replicate this study with high schools that include more male teachers in the Southeastern United States for more meaningful descriptions of the acculturation experiences faced by ELLs within the classroom learning environment.

The second recommendation is based on Research Question 2 and the findings of Constituent 1, providing a culturally relevant classroom learning environment. Dessie and Sewagegn (2019) emphasized the acculturation experiences and academic achievement of ELLs by creating culturally relevant classroom environments that are conducive to meeting the needs of ELLs. The second recommendation for future research is to replicate this study with high school ELLs for more meaningful descriptions of their acculturation experiences within the classroom learning environment in the United States. This qualitative descriptive phenomenological study aimed to provide meaningful descriptions of the ELLs' phenomenon (Maxwell, 2020). A qualitative method was the primary approach to describe truthfully and accurately the summation of the phenomenon (Anjum et al., 2020).

The third recommendation is based on Research Question 1 and the findings of Constituent 3, which are the academic disadvantages faced by ELLs within the classroom. For instance, ELLs face cultural disadvantages in their classroom (Stark et al., 2021). The third recommendation for future research studies could include a quantitative methodology. Quantitative methods aim to understand the relationships between variables (Hamilton & Finley, 2019; Maxwell, 2020). This recommendation could allow future researchers to use a larger sample, and the results could be more generalized. Future researchers could investigate the lived experiences of ELLs in the same region in the United States by using quantitative methods. The results may provide different perspectives on the acculturation experiences of ELLs within the classroom learning environment.

## Conclusions

The problem addressed by this study was the acculturation experiences of ELLs within the classroom learning environment in the United States (Bennouna et al., 2021; Hendy & Cuevas, 2020; Hong et al., 2019; Murray, 2020; Soland & Sandilos, 2021). The purpose of this qualitative, descriptive phenomenological study was to explore the acculturation experiences of ELLs within the classroom learning environment in the United States. A qualitative method was used to describe the acculturation experiences of ELLs within the classroom learning environment (Creswell, 2013, 2014). A qualitative method is aligned with Amedeo Giorgi's (2009) descriptive phenomenological design. Semi-structured interviews were conducted with eight participants. The participants described the acculturation experiences of ELLs within the classroom learning environment. The semi-structured interviews were transcribed, and then a member-checking process was used to ensure the accuracy of the transcripts. The data analysis was guided by Giorgi's (2009) analysis process. Therefore, Giorgi's (2009) five-step data analysis process was used to provide meaningful descriptions of the acculturation experiences of ELLs within the classroom learning environment from teachers' perspectives.

The findings of this study aligned with Berry's (1997) acculturation theory. Berry's (1997) acculturation theory focuses on describing the lived experiences of immigrants and their acculturation experiences to the host culture. All eight participants shared their experiences through three research questions. Nine constituents emerged from this qualitative, descriptive phenomenological data analysis. The constituents were ELLs disconnected from the classroom, English language barriers faced by ELLs, academic disadvantages faced by ELLs within the classroom, the challenges faced by ELLs to cope within the classroom, providing culturally relevant classroom learning environment, lack of teachers' awareness and classroom support, native language support and visual classroom presentations, creating a culturally inclusive classroom environment, and culturally classroom resources and bilingual support to help ELLs. Several meaningful constituents emerged and were supported by the literature review of this study. The findings of these constituents enhance the knowledge of Berry's (1997) acculturation theory.

The findings of this study revealed that ELLs struggle significantly and become more reserved in acclimating within the classroom learning environment. Therefore, it is crucial for ELLs to feel comfortable, feel safe, and become a part of the classroom learning environment. Also, participants shared that many teachers lack knowledge regarding ELLs' cultural backgrounds, there are insufficient bilingual personnel available in the classroom, a lack of cultural classroom resources, limited time, and an English language barrier between teachers and ELLs. Participants suggested that ELLs need culturally inclusive classrooms to overcome their challenges and assimilate into the new school culture environment. A culturally inclusive classroom creates a welcoming environment for ELLs. The study highlighted that teachers need additional classroom resources to meet the challenges ELLs encounter within the classroom learning environment. It requires many resources to meet the needs of ELLs. It requires a team. A team includes teachers, parents, community agencies, and school administrators to meet the needs of ELLs and provide emotional, social, and academic support to all ELLs. Future qualitative and quantitative research studies are suggested to explore the phenomenon of ELLs in the United States.

# REFERENCES

Abedi, J., Zhang, Y., Rowe, S. E., & Lee, H. (2020). Examining effectiveness and validity of accommodations for English language learners in mathematics: An evidence-based computer accommodation decision system. *Educational Measurement: Issues and Practice,*39(4), 41–52. https://doi.org/10.1111/emip.12328

Adams, D. L., & Hord, C. (2023). Preservice special education teachers' perceptions of field experience with English-language learner students. *Education Sciences, 13*(7), Article 726. https://doi.org/10.3390/educsci13070726

Agarkar, S. C. (2019). Influence of learning theories on science education. *Resonance: Journal of Science Education,* 24(8), 847–859. https://doi-org.lopes.idm.oclc.org/10.1007/s12045-019-0848-7

Åhs, J. W., Ranheim, A., Eriksson, H., & Mazaheri, M. (2023). Encountering suffering in digital care: A qualitative study of providers' experiences in telemental health care. *BMC Health Services Research, 23*(1), Article 41(8) https://doi.org/10.1186/s12913-023-09367-x

Al-Krenawi, A., Alotaibi, F., & Elbedour, S. (2021). Acculturative stress among female Saudi college students in the United States. *Community Mental Health Journal, 57*(2), 372–379. https://doi.org/10.1007/s10597-020-00659-8

Amaro-Jiménez, C., Hungerford-Kresser, H., Esquivel, S., Doddy, M., & Daniel, B. (2020). Partnering for change: lessons from college access efforts for culturally and linguistically diverse students and families. *School Community Journal, 30*(2), 105–120.

Andrei, E., & Northrop, L. (2022). Online resources and professional development for teachers of English learners: A US State-by-State Analysis. *TESL-EJ, 26*(3).

Anjum, A., Saeed Ali, T., Akber Pradhan, N., Khan, M., & Karmaliani, R. (2020). Perceptions of stakeholders about the role of health system in suicide prevention in Ghizer, Gilgit Baltistan, Pakistan. *BMC Public Health,* 20(1), 1–14. https://doi-org.lopes.idm.oclc.org/10.1186/s12889-020-09081-x

Antoniadou, M., & Quinlan, K. M. (2020). Thriving on challenges: how immigrant academics regulate emotional experiences during acculturation. *Studies in Higher Education,* 45(1), 71–85. https://doi.org/10.1080/03075079.2018.15512567

Arellano, B., Liu, F., Stoker, G., & Slama, R. (2018). *Initial Spanish proficiency and English language development among Spanish-speaking English learner students in New Mexico* (REL 2018–286). Washington, DC: U.S. Department of Education, Institute of Education Sciences, National Center for Education Evaluation and Regional Assistance, Regional Educational Laboratory.

Artigliere, M. (2019). The proficiency, instructional and affective domains of long term English language learners: A review of the research. *TESL-EJ, 23*(1), 1–19.

Astroth, K. S., & Chung, S. Y. (2018). Exploring the evidence quantitative and qualitative research: focusing on the fundamentals: Reading qualitative research with a critical eye. *Nephrology Nursing Journal, 45*(4), 381–386.

Balilah, A. M. A., & Archibald, L. M. D. (2022). Processing-dependent measures sensitive to language performance differences in Arabic-speaking English language learners compared to children with developmental language disorder. *Canadian Journal of Speech-Language Pathology & Audiology, 46*(3), 171–184.

Bal, N. G. (2022). Cultural intelligence of English language learners and their perceived strengths and weaknesses in intercultural communication. *TESL-EJ, 26*(2).

Belotto, M. J. (2018). Data analysis methods for qualitative research: managing the challenges of coding, interrater reliability, and thematic analysis. *The Qualitative Report,* 11, 2622.

Benbaba, A., & Lindner, J. (2023). Perceptions of barriers to learning management systems among teaching English to speakers of other languages teachers in Alabama and Mississippi. *Quarterly Review of Distance Education,* 24(1), 1–13.

Bennouna, C., Brumbaum, H., McLay, M. M., Allaf, C., Wessells, M., & Stark, L. (2021). The role of culturally responsive social and emotional learning in supporting refugee inclusion and belonging: A thematic analysis of service provider perspectives. *PLoS ONE,* 16(8), 1–19. https://doi.org/10.1371/journal.pone.0256743

Ben Salem, R., & Damak Ayadi, S. (2023). The impact of acculturation process and the institutional isomorphism on IFRS adoption. *EuroMed Journal of Business,* 18(2), 184–206. https://doi.org/10.1108/EMJB-04-2021-0058

Berry, J. W., & Hou, F. (2016). Immigrant acculturation and wellbeing in Canada. *Canadian Psychology/Psychologie Canadienne,* 57(4), 254.

Berry, J. W. (2005). Acculturation: Living successfully in two cultures. *International Journal of Intercultural Relations,* 29, 697-712. doi:10.1016/j.ijintrel.2005.07.013

Berry, J. W. (2015). Global psychology: Implications for cross-cultural research and management. *Cross Cultural Management,* 22(3), 342-355.

Berry, J. W. (1990). Psychology of acculturation: understanding individuals moving between cultures. *In R. Brislin (Ed.), Applied Cross-Cultural Psychology* (pp. 232–253). *Newbury, CA: Sage.*

Berry, J. W. (1997). Immigration, acculturation, and adaptation. *Applied Psychology,* 46, 5–34

Björling, E. A., Louie, B., Wiesmann, P., & Kuo, A. C. (2021). Engaging English language learners as cultural informants in the design of a social robot for education. *Multimodal Technologies and Interaction,* 5(7), 35.

Boileau, L. L. A., Bless, H., & Gebauer, J. E. (2022). The 'mixed bag' of segregation—on positive and negative associations with migrants' acculturation. *European Journal of Social Psychology.* https://doi.org/10.1002/ejsp.2830

Bowers, J. M., Hamilton, J. G., Wu, Y. P., Moyer, A., & Hay, J. L. (2022). Acculturation, sun tanning behavior, and tanning attitudes among Asian college students in the Northeastern USA. *International Journal of Behavioral Medicine,* 29(1), 25–35. https://doi.org/10.1007/s12529-021-09993-x

Bullard, E. (2019). Purposive sampling. Salem Press Encyclopedia.

Buono, S., & Jang, E. E. (2021). The effect of linguistic factors on assessment of English language learners' mathematical ability: A differential item functioning analysis. *Educational Assessment,* 26(2), 125–144. https://doi.org/10.1080/10627197.2020.1858783

Burn, K., & Menter, I. (2021). Making sense of teacher education in a globalizing world: The distinctive contribution of a sociocultural approach. *Comparative Education Review*, 65(4), 770–789. https://doi.org/10.1086/716228

Cai, J., Wen, Q., Lombaerts, K., Jaime, I., & Cai, L. (2022). Assessing students' perceptions about classroom learning environments: the new what is happening in this class (NWI-HIC) instrument. learning environments research: *An International Journal*, 25(2), 601–618. https://doi.org/10.1007/s10984-021-09383-w

Camping, A., Graham, S., & Harris, K. R. (2023). Writing motives and writing achievement of elementary school students from diverse language backgrounds. *Journal of Educational Psychology*, 115(7), 1028–1043. https://doi.org/10.1037/edu0000796.

Casey, J. E., Linn, D., Pennington, L. K., Mireles, S. V., & Lopez, D. J. (2020). Modified literature circle: Incorporating English and Spanish picturebooks to support English language learners during a fifth-grade science lesson. *Texas Journal of Literacy Education*, 8(2), 62–75.

Castleberry, A., & Nolen, A. (2018). Thematic analysis of qualitative research data: Is it as easy as it sounds? *Currents in Pharmacy Teaching and Learning*, 10(6), 807–815. https://doi-org.lopes.idm.oclc.org/10.1016/j.cptl.2018.03.019

Castro Olivo, S. M., Ura, S., & dAbreu, A. (2022). The effects of a culturally adapted program on ELL students' core SEL competencies as measured by a modified version of the BERS-2. *Journal of Applied School Psychology*, 38(4), 380-396.

Cho, H., Wang, X. C., & Christ, T. (2019). Social-emotional learning of refugee English language learners in early elementary grades: Teachers' perspectives. *Journal of Research in Childhood Education, 33*(1), 40-55.

Choy, B., Arunachalam, K., Gupta S, Taylor, M., & Lee, A. (2021). Systematic review: Acculturation strategies and their impact on the mental health of migrant populations. *Public Health in Practice*, 2(100069-). https://doi.org/10.1016/j.puhip.2020.100069

Cömert, M. (2018). A qualitative research on the contribution of in-service training to the vocational development of teachers. *Journal of Education and Training Studies*, 6(7), 114–129.

Creswell, J.W. (2013). *Qualitative inquiry and research design: Choosing among five approaches.* Sage Publications.

Creswell, J. W. (2014). *Research design: Qualitative, quantitative, and mixed methods approaches.* Sage publications.

Creswell, L., & Cage, E. (2019). 'Who am I?' an exploratory study of the relationships between identity, acculturation and mental health in autistic adolescents. *Journal of Autism and Developmental Disorders, 49*(7), 2901-2912.

Danford, C. A. (2023). Understanding the evidence: Qualitative research designs. *Urologic Nursing*, 43(1), 41–45. https://doi.org/10.7257/2168-4626.2023.43.1.41

Dang, T. K. A., Carbone, A., Ye, J., & Vu, T. T. P. (2022). How academics manage individual differences to team teach in higher education: A sociocultural activity theory perspective. *Higher Education* (00181560), 84(2), 415–434. https://doi.org/10.1007/s10734-021-00777-6

Davis, T., & Tesh, G. (2022). English language learners' experience with learning management systems. *International Journal of TESOL Studies*, 4(3), 66. https://doi.org/10.46451/ijts.2022.03.06 de Araujo, Z., & Smith, E. (2022). Examining English language learners' learning needs through the lens of algebra curriculum materials. *Educational Studies in Mathematics*, 109(1), 65–87. https://doi.org/10.1007/s10649-021-10081-w

Delgado, R. K. G., & Sun, Q. (2022). Challenges, changes, and choices: Immigrant academics of color in american academia. *Adult Learning*, 33(3), 114–122. https://doi.org/10.1177/1045159521997583

Dessie, A. A., & Sewagegn, A. A. (2019). Moving beyond a sign of judgment: Primary school teachers' perception and practice of feedback. *International Journal of Instruction*, 12(2), 51–66.

de Valenzuela, J. S., Pacheco, R., & Shenoy, S. (2022). Current practices and challenges in language proficiency assessment for English learners with complex support needs. *Research & Practice for Persons with Severe Disabilities*, 47(1), 6–21. https://doi.org/10.1177/15407969221075848

Dewi, R. S., Fitriah, S., Nahartini, D., Setiyaningsih, S., & Fachrurrozi. (2021). Indonesian migrant workers' language and cultural barriers in accessing health care system in foreign countries. *Turkish Online Journal of Qualitative Inquiry*, 12(3), 1995–2020.

Donate, M. M., Rodríguez, C. T., Rodríguez, A. J., Hernández, M. A., Santos, H. G., & Beato, F. L. (2021). Mixed-method study of women's assessment and experience of childbirth care. *Journal of Advanced Nursing (John Wiley & Sons, Inc.)*, 77(10), 4195–4210. https://doi.org/10.1111/jan.14984

Duran, C. A. (2022). A Phenomenological study on the lived experiences of grade 4 teachers in the transition of medium of instruction. *International Journal of Early Childhood Special Education*, 14(6), 1778–1790. https://doi.org/10.9756/INTJECSE/V14I6.215

Dursun, F., & Sevim, Ö. M. (2022). Receiving education in a different country: Challenges encountered by foreign students and proposed solutions. *Acta Educationis Generalis*, 12(2), 140–162. https://doi.org/10.2478/atd-2022-0018

Ellis, P. (2021). Sampling in qualitative research (3). Wounds UK, 17(1), 128–130.

Fang, L. (2020). Acculturation and academic achievement of rural to urban migrant youth: The role of school satisfaction and family closeness. *International Journal of Intercultural Relations*, 74, 149–160. https://doi.org/10.1016/j.ijintrel.2019.11.006

Filia, K. M., Jackson, H. J., Cotton, S. M., Gardner, A., & Killackey, E. J. (2018). What is social inclusion? A thematic analysis of professional opinion. *Psychiatric Rehabilitation Journal*, 41(3), 183–195. https://doi-org.lopes.idm.oclc.org/10.1037/prj000030.

Flynn, R., Albrecht, L., & Scott, S. D. (2018). Two approaches to focus group data collection for qualitative health research. *International Journal of Qualitative Methods*, 17(1). https://doi.org/10.1177/1609406917750781

Fofana, F., Bazeley, P., & Regnault, A. (2020). Applying a mixed methods design to test saturation for qualitative data in health outcomes research. *PLoS ONE*, 15(6), 1–12. https://doi.org/10.1371/journal.pone.0234898

Gagné, M., & Deci, E. L. (2005). Self-determination theory and work motivation. *Journal of Organizational Behavior*, 26(4), 331-331+. http://dx.doi.org/10.1002/job.322

Garcia-Borrego, R., Maxwell, G. M., & McNair, C. L. (2020). South Texas urban administrator perceptions of best practices for ELL literacy. *Journal of Instructional Pedagogies, 23*

Garcia, E. B., Sulik, M. J., & Obradović, J. (2019). Teachers' perceptions of students' executive functions: disparities by gender, ethnicity, and ELL status. *Journal of Educational Psychology.* doi:10.1037/edu0000308

Gilblom, E. A., Crary, S. L., & Sang, H. I. (2022). "We wanna feel like we are America": examining the inclusive and exclusionary high school experiences of new Americans in a small city. *International Journal of Multicultural Education*, 24(3), 30–50. https://doi.org/10.18251/ijme.v24i3.3201

Giles, A., & Yazan, B. (2020). "You're Not an Island": A middle grades language arts teacher's changed perceptions in ESL and content teachers' collaboration. RMLE online: *Research in Middle Level Education,* 43(3). https://doi.org/10.1080/19404476.2020.1724045

Giorgi, A. (2009). Descriptive phenomenological method in psychology: Husserlian approaches. *New York: Duquesne University Press.*

Goldman, J. A., Heddy, B. C., & Laird, S. (2018). An interdisciplinary discourse between Dewey and self-determination theory: Motivation in the wake of monetizing education. *Education and Culture*, 34(2), 89. https://doi-org.lopes.idm.oclc.org/10.5703/education culture.34.2.0089 (1), 191. https://doi-org.lopes.idm.oclc.org/10.1111/1467-8551.12262

Gordon, M. M. (1964). *Assimilation in American Life.* New York: Oxford University Press.

Grenz, G., Chitiyo, G., & Fidan, P. (2023). Perceptions of teachers towards English language learners (ELLs) and content accessibility. *International Journal of Research in Education and Science* (IJRES), 9(3), 823-835. https://doi.org/10.46328/ijres.3225

Guler, N. (2020). Preparing to teach English language learners: Effect of online courses in changing mainstream teachers' perceptions of English language learners. *Innovation in Language Learning and Teaching,* 14(1), 83-96.

Guo, M., Stensland, M., Li, M., Beck, T., & Dong, X. (2020). Transition in older parent–adult child relations in US Chinese immigrant families. *The Gerontologist*, 60(2), 302-312.

Gupta, A. (2019). Principles and practices of teaching English language learners. *International Education Studies,* 12(7), 49-57.

Hamilton, A. B., & Finley, E. P. (2020). Reprint of: Qualitative methods in implementation research: An introduction psychiatry research. *Research in Childhood Education,* 33(1), 40-55.

Hanfstingl, B., Arzenšek, A., Apschner, J., & Gölly, K. I. (2021). Assimilation and accommodation: A systematic review of the last two decades. *European Psychologist.*

Hansson, T., Andersson, M. E., Ahlström, G., & Hansson, S. R. (2022). Women's experiences of preeclampsia as a condition of uncertainty: A qualitative study. *BMC Pregnancy and Childbirth,* 22(1). https://doi.org/10.1186/s12884-022-04826-5

Hartshorne, J. K., Tenenbaum, J. B., & Pinker, S. (2018). A critical period for second language acquisition: Evidence from 2/3 million English speakers. *Cognition,* 177, 263-277. https://doi.org/10.1016/j.cognition.2018.04.007

Hawkins, M. M., Holliday, D. D., Weinhardt, L. S., Florsheim, P., Ngui, E., & AbuZahra, T. (2022). Barriers and facilitators of health among older adult immigrants in the United States: An integrative review of 20 years of literature. BMC Public Health, 22(1), 1–17. https://doi.org/10.1186/s12889-022-13042-x

Helmich, E., Stenfors, T., & Barrett, A. (2018). How to…choose between different types of data. *Clinical Teacher*, 15(5), 366–369. https://doi-org.lopes.idm.oclc.org/10.1111/tct.12925

Hendy, E., & Cuevas, J. (2020). The Effects on instructional conversations on English language learners. *Georgia Educational Researcher*, 17(2).

Hennink, M., & Kaiser, B. N. (2022). Sample sizes for saturation in qualitative research: A systematic review of empirical tests. *Social Science & Medicine*, 292, N.PAG. https://doi.org/10.1016/j.socscimed.2021.114523

Hieu Van Ngo. (2023). The differential experience and educational outcomes among two cohorts of English language learning students. *Alberta Journal of Educational Research*, 69(1), 66–85.

Hong, H., Keith, K., & Moran, R. R. (2019). Reflection on and for Actions: Probing into English language art teachers' personal and professional experiences with English language learners. *TESL-EJ*, 22(4).

Horne, O. (2021). Interventions for English Language Learners: A Review. *Vanderbilt Undergraduate Research Journal*, 11.

Howson, A. (2019). Qualitative research methods sociology. *Salem Press Encyclopedia*

Hsin, L., Rapaport, A., Osman, D., Kilborn, M., Pierson, A., & Garrett, R. (2022). English proficiency and the pandemic: How Texas English learner students fared during the COVID-19 pandemic. REL 2023-144. *In Regional Educational Laboratory Southwest. Regional Educational Laboratory Southwest.*.

Huang, J. (2022). Task-based language teaching and rigorous instruction in beginning English as a second language classrooms. *New Directions for Adult & Continuing Education*, 2022(175/176), 59–70. https://doi.org/10.1002/ace.20468

Huck, C. (2021). Policy Brief: Improving graduation rates and postsecondary outcomes for English learners in Florida. *NABE Journal of Research and Practice*, 11(1–2), 46–52. https://doi.org/10.1080/26390043.2021.1977594

Hussain, M. S., Salam, A., & Farid, A. (2020). Students' motivation in English language learning (ELL): An exploratory study of motivation-al factors for EFL and ESL adult learners. *International Journal of Applied Linguistics and English Literature*, 9(4), 15-28.

Ibrahim, R. (2023). Investigating preservice teachers' self-efficacy and motivation to teach English language learners (ELLs). *International Journal of Modern Education Studies*, 7(1), 75–105. https://doi.org/10.51383/ijonmes.2023.293

Irby, B. J., Tong, F., Lara-Alecio, R., Guerrero, C., Guo, W., Abdelrahman, N., & Serrano, J. (2020). Teacher perceptions of the effectiveness of a science-infused literacy intervention for English language learners. Pedagogies: *An International Journal*, 15(1), 18–39. https://doi.org/10.1080/1554480X.2019.1673165

Irvine, J. (2018). A Framework for comparing theories related to motivation in education. *Research in Higher Education Journal*, 35.

Jackson, C., Vaughan, D. R., & Brown, L. (2018). Discovering lived experiences through descriptive phenomenology. *International Journal of Contemporary Hospitality Management*, 30(11), 3309-3325.

Johnson, A. M., & Thorne-Wallington, E. (2021). From theory to implementation: Examining EL certification requirements through the lens of local context. *Education Policy Analysis Archives*, 29(103–105), 1–32. https://doi.org/10.14507/epaa.29.5253

Jones, L., O'Connor, E., & Boag, H. C. (2018). International psychology students use multiple strengths to enhance their learning and performance on work placements. *Australian Psychologist, 53*(6), 505–516. https://doi-org.lopes.idm.oclc.org/10.1111/ap.12351

Kapoyannis, T. (2021). The name jar project: supporting preservice teachers in working with English language learners. Language & literacy: *A Canadian Educational E-Journal, 23*(3), 45–65. https://doi.org/10.20360/langandlit29510

Karimi, S., Haghani, F., Yamani, N., & Kalyani, M. N. (2017). Exploring the perception of nursing students about consequences of reflection in clinical settings. *Electronic Physician, 9*(9), 5191–5198. https://doi-org.lopes.idm.oclc.org/10.19082/5191

Karimi, Z., Fereidouni, Z., Behnammoghadam, M., Alimohammadi, N., Mousavizadeh, A., Salehi, T., & Mirzaee, S. (2020). The lived experience of nurses caring for patients with COVID-19 in Iran: a phenomenological study. *Risk management and healthcare policy,* 1271-1278.

Kennedy, C., & McLoughlin, A. (2023). Developing the emergent literacy skills of English language learners through dialogic reading: A Systematic review. *Early Childhood Education Journal, 51*(2), 317–332. https://doi.org/10.1007/s10643-021-01291-1

Khawaja, N. G., & Carr, K. (2020). Exploring the factor structure and psychometric properties of an acculturation and resilience scale with culturally and linguistically diverse adolescents. *Australian Psychologist, 55*(1), 26–37. https://doi.org/10.1111/ap.12436

Khoo, E., & Kang, S. (2022). Proactive learner empowerment: towards a transformative academic integrity approach for English language learners. *International Journal for Educational Integrity, 18*(1), 1–24. https://doi.org/10.1007/s40979-022-00111-2

Koketso, M. F., Calvin, M. J., Lehlokwe, S. I., & Mafa, P. (2019). Perspectives of single mothers on the socio-emotional and economic influence of "absent fathers" in child's life: A case study of rural community in South Africa. *E-BANGI Journal, 16*(4), 1–12.

Kraus, E. S. (2023). Developing intercultural competencies: The roles and responsibilities of native English-speaking teachers (NESTs). *International Forum of Teaching & Studies, 19*(1), 25–43.

Krsmanovic, M. (2020). "I was new and i was afraid": The acculturation strategies adopted by international first-year undergraduate students in the United States. *Journal of International Students, 10*(4), 954–975.

Kumi-Yeboah, A., Brobbey, G., & Smith, P. (2020). Exploring factors that facilitate acculturation strategies and academic success of West African immigrant youth in urban schools. *Education and Urban Society, 52*(1), 21-50.

Kvale, S. (1999). The psychoanalytic interview as qualitative research. *Qualitative Inquiry, 5*(1), 87–113.

Lai, H., Wang, D., & Ou, X. (2023). Cross-cultural adaptation of Chinese students in the United States: Acculturation strategies, sociocultural, psychological, and academic adaptation. *Frontiers in Psychology, 14,* 01-13. https://doi.org/10.3389/fpsyg.2022.924561

LaScotte, D. (2020). Leveraging listening texts in vocabulary acquisition for low-literate learners. (perspectives). *TESL Canada Journal, 37*(1), NA. https://doi.org/10.18806/tesl.v37i1.1330

Lee, E. N., & Orgill, M. (2022). Toward equitable assessment of English language learners in general chemistry: Identifying supportive features in assessment items. *Journal of Chemical Education*, 99(1), 35–48. https://doi.org/10.1021/acs.jchemed.1c00370

Lee, E. N., Orgill, M., & Kardash, C. (2020). Supporting English language learners in college science classrooms: Insights from chemistry students. *Multicultural Education*, 27(3–4), 25–32.

Lee, E., Subramaniam, K., & Castro, D. C. (2023). Early Childhood pre-service teacher's descriptions of equity in science education: A thematic analysis. *Early childhood Education Journal*, 51(3), 483–492. https://doi.org/10.1007/s10643-022-01318-1

Lewis, K. D., & Brown, S. L. (2021). College ready or not? Engaging and supporting English language learners in higher education. *Journal of Effective Teaching in Higher Education*, 4(1), 109-127.

Liaqat, A., Munteanu, C., & Demmans Epp, C. (2021). Collaborating with mature English language learners to combine peer and automated feedback: A user-centered approach to designing writing support. *International Journal of Artificial Intelligence in Education (Springer Science & Business Media B.V.)*, 31(4), 638–679. https://doi.org/10.1007/s40593-020-00204-4

Liestøl, G. (2019). Augmented reality storytelling: narrative design and reconstruction of a historical event in situ. *International Journal of Interactive Mobile Technologies*, 13(12), 196–209.

Li, G., & Jee, Y. (2021). Pan-diversity integration as an equity trap: Lessons from preservice teachers' preparation for teaching English language learners in a predominantly white institution in the United States. *Teachers College Record*, 123(12), 125–154. https://doi.org/10.1177/01614681211070873

Lim, N., O'Reilly, M. F., Londono, F. V., & Russell-George, A. (2021). Overcoming language barriers between interventionists and immigrant parents of children with autism spectrum disorder. *Journal of Autism & Developmental Disorders*, 51(8), 2876–2890. https://doi.org/10.1007/s10803-020-04754-3

Lincoln, Y. S., & Guba, E. G. (1986). But is it rigorous? trustworthiness and authenticity in naturalistic evaluation. *New Directions for Program Evaluation*, 30, 73–84.

Liu, S., He, L., Wei, M., Du, Y., & Cheng, D. (2022). Depression and anxiety from acculturative stress: Maladaptive perfectionism as a mediator and mindfulness as a moderator. *Asian American Journal of Psychology*, 13(2), 207.

Lomotey, A. Y., Bam, V., Diji, A. K. A., Asante, E., Asante, H. B., & Osei, J. (2020). Experiences of mothers with preterm babies at a mother and baby unit of a tertiary hospital: A descriptive phenomenological study. *Nursing Open*, 7(1), 150-159.

Lowenhaupt, R., Bradley, S., & Dallas, J. (2020). The (re)classification of English learners: A district case study of identification, integration, and the design of services. *Leadership & Policy in Schools*, 19(1), 60–80. https://doi.org/10.1080/15700763.2020.1714056

Lumbrears, R., & Rupley, W. H. (2019). Educational experiences of ELL educators: Searching for instructional insights to promote ELL students' learning. *Educational Research for Policy and Practice*, 18, 17-38.

Luo, M., Zhang, X., Peng, F., Zhao, J., & Deng, H. (2021). Predictors of acculturation attitude of international students in China. *PLoS ONE*, 16(11). https://doi.org/10.1371/journal.pone.0260616

Maarouf, S. A. (2019). Supporting academic growth of English language learners: Integrating reading into stem curriculum. *World Journal of Education*, 9(4), 83–96. https://eds-b-ebscohost-com.lopes.idm.oclc.org/eds/detail/detail?

Madler, A. M., Anderson, S. K., LeMire, S. D., & Smith, K. (2022). Perceptions of teacher preparation for classroom diversity. *Mid-Western Educational Researcher*, 34(1), 42–68.

Mardian, F., & Nafissi, Z. (2022). Synchronous computer-mediated corrective feedback and EFL learners' grammatical knowledge development: A sociocultural perspective. *Iranian Journal of Language Teaching Research*, 10(2), 115–136.

Mašková, I., & Kučera, D. (2022). Performance, achievement, and success in psychological research: Towards a more transparent use of the still ambiguous terminology. *Psychological Reports*, 125(2), 1218–1261. https://doi.org/10.1177/0033294121996000

Maxwell, J. A. (2020). Why qualitative methods are necessary for generalization. *Qualitative Psychology*. https://doi-org.lopes.idm.oclc.org/10.1037/qup0000173

Ma, Z., & Xia, Y. (2021). Acculturation strategies, age at migration, and self-rated health: An empirical study on internal migrants in China. *Social Science Research*, 93. https://doi.org/10.1016/j.ssresearch.2020.102487

McGregor, J., & Tsosie, R. (2021). Rethinking research protections for tribal communities. *American Journal of Bioethics*, 21(10), 30–32. https://doi.org/10.1080/15265161.2021.1965244

Meng, C. (2020). Effect of classroom language diversity on head start ELL and non-ELL children's social-emotional development. *Applied Developmental Science*, 24(3), 230–241. https://doi.org/10.1080/10888691.2018.1461015

Mills, T., Villegas, A. M., & Cochran-Smith, M. (2020). Research on preparing preservice mainstream teachers for linguistically diverse classrooms. *Teacher Education Quarterly*, 47(4), 33–55.

Min, M., Whitehead, A., Wells, C., & Akerson V. (2023). Unpacking elementary preservice teachers' beliefs on culturally and linguistically responsive mathematics and science teaching for English language learners. *International Journal of Research in Education and Science (IJRES)*, 9(2), 444-460. https://doi.org/10.46328/ijres.3068

Montgomery, G., Zhang, Y. B., & Imamura, M. (2021). The effects of Latino immigrants' acculturation strategy and U.S. Americans' assimilation attitudes on perceptions of accommodation satisfaction and willingness to communicate. *International Journal of Intercultural Relations*, 82, 157–167. https://doi.org/10.1016/j.ijintrel.2021.03.008

Moussa, N. M. (2021). International students' achievements and adaptation to the United States' culture. *Qualitative Research Journal*, 21(4), 498–512. https://doi.org/10.1108/QRJ-11-2020-0145

Murphy, A. F., & Torff, B. (2019). Teachers' beliefs about rigor of curriculum for English language learners. *Educational Forum*, 83(1), 90–101.

Murphy, A. F., Torff, B., & Sessions, D. (2019). Educators' beliefs about appropriate pedagogical models for Spanish-speaking ELLs who differ in home-language and English-language literacy abilities in the United States. *International Journal of Bilingual Education & Bilingualism*, 22(4), 402.

Murray, B. P. (2020). Language and adjustment anxieties of first-year college student English language learners. *Journal of Behavioral & Social Sciences*, 7(2), 119–136.

Nerlinger, S. J. (2021). The bilingual dictionary accommodation: Can it help your students succeed on tests? *NABE Journal of Research and Practice*, 11(1–2), 22–31. https://doi.org/10.1080/26390043.2021.1962227

Nguyen, A. M., & Rule, N. O. (2020). Implicit biculturalism theories: How bicultural individuals perceive others and organize their own cultures. *Identity*, 20(4), 258-271.

Nigar, N. (2020). Hermeneutic phenomenological narrative enquiry: A qualitative study design. *Theory and Practice in Language Studies*, 10(1), 10.

Noor, Q., Basit, A., Arif, M. I., Iftikhar, H., & Khalid, N. (2021). Effect of classroom learning environment on students' achievement motivation at university level. *Turkish Online Journal of Qualitative Inquiry*, 12(10), 5246–5259.

O'Brien, B., Tuohy, D., Fahy, A., & Markey, K. (2019). Home students' experiences of intercultural learning: A qualitative descriptive design. *Nurse Education Today*, 74, 25–30. https://doi-org.lopes.idm.oclc.org/10.1016/j.nedt.2018.12.005

Olds, J., McCraney, M., Panesar-Aguilar, S., & Cale, C. (2021). Adopting instructional strategies for English language learners in elementary classrooms. *World Journal of Education*, 11(3), 18–29.

Olifant, T., Cekiso, M., & Rautenbach, E. (2019). Teachers' perceptions of Grades 8–10 English First additional language learners' reading habits, attitudes and motivation. *Reading & Writing*, (1), e1. https://doi-org.lopes.idm.oclc.org/10.4102/rw.v10i1.254

Owens, C. W., & Wells, S. P. (2021). Elementary content teacher perceptions regarding their ELL instructional practices. *Journal of Educational Research & Practice*, 11(1), 139–152. https://doi.org/10.5590/JERAP.2020.11.1.10

Pacheco, E.-M. (2020). Culture learning theory and globalization: Reconceptualizing culture shock for modern cross-cultural sojourners. *New Ideas in Psychology*, 58. https://doi.org/10.1016/j.newideapsych.2020.100801

Panunciar, D. M., Poculan, C. M., & Pogoy, A. M. (2022). Remote students lived experiences in distance learning. *International Journal of Early Childhood Special Education*, 14(5), 6245–6255. https://doi.org/10.9756/INTJECSE/V14I5.776

Parker, M. M., Das, B., & Kelly, C. T. (2021). Latinx students' perceptions of school counseling activities: a content analysis. *Journal of School Counseling*, 19(40), 1–35.

Pendakur, R. (2021). Settlement and labour force outcomes for Afghan immigrants and their children in Canada. *Journal of Ethnic & Migration Studies*, 47(21), 4893–4913. https://doi.org/10.1080/1369183X.2020.1724423

Protacio, S., Piazza, S. V., David, V., & Tigchelaar, M. (2020). Elementary teachers' initiatives in engaging families of English learners. *School Community Journal*, 30(2), 211–227.

Redfield, R., Linton, R., & Herskovits, M.J. (1936). Memorandum for the study of acculturation. *American Anthropologist*, 38, 149–152. https://doi.org/10.1525/aa.1936.38.1.02a00330

Rivaz, M., Shokrollahi, P., & Ebadi, A. (2019). Online focus group discussions: An attractive approach to data collection for qualitative health research. *Nursing Practice Today*, 6(1), 413–415.

Rodriguez, A. J., Quero Palomino, M. A., Aznar Sepulveda, E., Fernandez, E. R. M. D. M., Ortiz Fernandez, F., Soto Barrera, V., & Hernandez, M. A. (2019). Experience of care through patients, family members and health professionals in an intensive care unit: A qualitative descriptive study. *Scandinavian Journal of Caring Sciences*, 33(4), 912–920. https://doi.org/10.1111/scs.12689

Roman Jr., R., & Nunez, A. M. (2020). Motivational factors that influence English as a foreign language learners at quality leadership university, Panama City, Panama. *Journal of Language Teaching & Research*, 11(4), 543–554. https://doi.org/10.17507/jltr.1104.03

Roudsari, R. L. (2019). Qualitative description: A less sophisticated approach for junior qualitative researchers. *Journal of Midwifery & Reproductive Health*, 7(4), 1856–1857. https://doi-org.lopes.idm.oclc.org/10.22038/jmrh.2019.13927

Sabidalas, M. A., & Esparar, J. (2022). Unfolding the saga of online ESL teachers: A descriptive phenomenological study. Psychology and education: *A Multidisciplinary Journal*, 5(9), 701-709.

Saito, K., Dewaele, J., Abe, M., & In'nami, Y. (2018). Motivation, emotion, learning experience, and second language comprehensibility development in classroom settings: A cross sectional and longitudinal study. *Language Learning*.doi10.1111/lang.12297.

Scharp, K. M., & Sanders, M. L. (2019). What is a theme? teaching thematic analysis in qualitative communication research methods. *Communication Teacher,* 33(2), 117–121.

Schneider, E., & Kulmhofer-Bommer, A. (2022). Let's play: Building oral competencies of English learners in k-3 settings through playful activities. *Dimensions of Early Childhood*, 50(1), 19–27.

Schumann, J. H. (1978). The Pagination Process: A Model for Second Language Acquisition. *Rowley, MA*: Newbury House.

Seixas, B. V., Smith, N., & Mitton, C. (2018). The qualitative descriptive approach in international comparative studies: Using online qualitative surveys. *International Journal of Health Policy and Management,* (9), 778. https://doi-org.lopes.idm.oclc.org/10.15171/IJHPM.2017.142

Shahbazi, S. (2020). Finding the right fit: exploring ESL teachers and students' perceptions of iLit ELL, a technology-based literacy program's use with high school English language learners. *International Journal of E-Learning & Distance Education*, 35(1), 1–34.

Shekhar, P., Prince, M., Finelli, C., Demonbrun, M., & Waters, C. (2019). Integrating quantitative and qualitative research methods to examine student resistance to active learning. *European Journal of Engineering Education*, 44(1), 6–18. https://doi-org.lopes.idm.oclc.org/doi:10.1080/03043797.2018.1438988.

Shi, H. (2018). English language learners' strategy use and self-efficacy beliefs in English language learning. *Journal of International Student*. 8 (2). 724-74, http://jistudents.org/doi:10.5281/zenodo.1250375.

Shim, J. M., & Shur, A. M. (2018). Learning from ELLs' perspectives: mismatch between

ELL and teacher perspectives on ELL learning experiences. *Canadian Center of Science and Education.* http://doi.org/10.5539/elt.v11n1p21.

Shorey, S., & Ng, E. D. (2022). Examining characteristics of descriptive phenomenological nursing studies: A scoping review. *Journal of Advanced Nursing,* 78(7), 1968-1979

Sim, J., Saunders, B., Waterfield, J., & Kingstone, T. (2018). Can sample size in qualitative research be determined a priori? *International Journal of Social Research Methodology*, 21(5), 619–634. https://doi-org.lopes.idm.oclc.org/10.1080/13645579.2018.1454643

Singer, N. (2022). Cartoons as the incidental vocabulary acquisition tool for English language learners. *Arab World English Journal (AWEJ)* Volume, 13. Sinha, R. (2021). Teaching English to ESL young learners: The use of activity-based learning as a teaching strategy. *Ilkogretim Online*, 20(4), 1136–1140. https://doi.org/10.17051/ilkon line.2021.04.126

Sirisha, I. (2018). Everyday problems in teaching English language to young learners. *Language in India,* 18(6).

Soland, J., & Sandilos, L. E. (2021). English language learners, self-efficacy, and the achievement gap: Understanding the relationship between academic and social-emotional growth. *Journal of Education for Students Placed at Risk*, 26(1), 20–44. https://doi.org/10.1080/10824669.2020.1787171.

Solmaz, O. (2020). Examining the collaborative reading experiences of English language learners for online second language socialization. *The Reading Matrix*: *An International Online Journal*, 20(1), 20-35.

Song, S. (2022). Digital service-learning: Creating translanguaging spaces for emergent bilinguals' literacy learning and culturally responsive family engagement in mainstream preservice teacher education. *TESL-EJ, 26(3)*.

Sousa, L. P. de Q., Tiraboschi, F. F., Lago, N. A. do, & Figueiredo, F. J. Q. de. (2019). Collaborative English language learning: Some reflections from interactions between Pairs. *Trabalhos Em Linguística Aplicada*, 58(1). https://doi.org/10.1590/010318138653439430941

Stairs-Davenport, A. (2023). "Where do i start?" inquiry into k-12 mainstream teachers' knowledge about differentiating instruction for ELLs in one US school district. *Education Inquiry*, 14(2), 163-177.

Stark, L., Robinson, M. V., Gillespie, A., Aldrich, J., Hassan, W., Wessells, M., Allaf, C., & Bennouna, C. (2021). Supporting mental health and psychosocial wellbeing through social and emotional learning: A participatory study of conflict-affected youth resettled to the U.S. *BMC Public Health*, 21(1), 1620. https://doi.org/10.1186/s12889-021-11674-z

Stavropoulou, A., Rovithis, M., Sigala, E., Moudatsou, M., Fasoi, G., Papageorgiou, D., & Koukouli, S. (2022). Exploring nurses' working experiences during the first wave of COVID-19 Outbreak. *Healthcare* (2227-9032), 10(8), 1406–N.PAG. https://doi.org/10.3390/healthcare10081406

Te Lindert, A., Korzilius, H. P., Stupar-Rutenfrans, S., & Van de Vijver, F. J. (2022). The role of perceived discrimination, intergroup contact and adoption in acculturation among four Dutch immigrant groups. *International Journal of Intercultural Relations*, 91, 297-310.

Sun, Y., & Gao, F. (2020). An investigation of the influence of intrinsic motivation on students' intention to use mobile devices in language learning. *Educational Technology Research & Development*, 68(3), 1181–1198. https://doi.org/10.1007/s11423-019-09733-9

Szymanski, A., & Lynch, M. (2020). Educator perceptions of English language learners. *Journal of Advanced Academics*, 31(4), 436–450. https://doi-org.lopes.idm.o-clc.org/10.1177/1932202X20917141

Theofanidis, D., & Fountouki, A. (2018). Limitations and delimitations in the research process. *Perioperative Nursing, 7*(3), 155–163. https://doi-org.lopes.idm.oclc.org/10.5281/zenodo.2552022

Tudy, R. A., & Gauran-Tudy, I. (2020). Struggles, coping mechanisms, and insights of childless teachers in the Philippines: A descriptive phenomenological approach. *The Qualitative Report, 25*(5), 1256-1278.

Turale, S. (2020). A Brief introduction to qualitative description: A research design worth using. *Pacific Rim International Journal of Nursing Research, 24*(3), 289–291.

Ugurel Kamisli, M. (2021). Acculturation experiences of Syrian Muslim refugee women in the United States: Intersectionality of nationality, religion, gender, and refugee status. *Adult Learning, 32*(3), 103-114.

Vasileiou, K., Barnett, J., Thorpe, S., & Terry Young, T. (2018). Characterizing and justifying sample size sufficiency in interview-based studies: Systematic analysis of qualitative health research over a 15-year period. *BMC Medical Research Methodology*, (1), 1. https://doi-org.lopes.idm.oclc.org/10.1186/s12874-018-0594-7.

Wang, X. & Yu, L. (2021). From the high school journal editorial board: Living in an anti-globalization era: A call for promoting critical multiculturalism and multicultural education for immigrant teachers and students in secondary education. *High School Journal, 104*(2), 79–83. https://doi.org/10.1353/hsj.2021.0002

Watanabe, T. (2022). How to develop phenomenology as psychology: From description to elucidation, exemplified based on a study of dream analysis. *Integrative Psychological & Behavioral Science, 56*(4), 964–980. https://doi.org/10.1007/s12124-020-09581-w

Watkinson, J. S., Shi, Q., Slezak, H., & Litvin, R. (2022). Preparing future school counselors to work with English language learners. *Journal of counselor preparation and supervision, 16*(1), 6.

Wei, L. (2021). Teaching academic vocabulary to English language learners (ELLs). *Theory and Practice in Language Studies*, 11(12), 1507-1514.

Wong, R., & Luo, Y. (2021). Relationship between learning motivation and learner autonomy among Chinese English language university students. *The Irish Journal of Education/Iris Eireannach an Oideachais*, 44, 1–22

Wood, A. E., & Mattson, C. A. (2019). Quantifying the effects of various factors on the utility of design ethnography in the developing world. *Research in Engineering Design, 30(3)*,317–338. https://doi-org.lopes.idm.oclc.org/10.1007/s00163-018-00304-2

Yamauchi, L. A., Soga, C. L., & Char, S. M. (2022). Professional development to improve interactions with culturally and linguistically diverse children: Reflections on practice. *Journal of Early Childhood Teacher Education, 43*(3), 426–449. https://doi.org/10.1080/10901027.2022.2032491

Yingling Lou. (2023). The cross-cultural experiences of international secondary students in anglophone countries--a hermeneutic literature review and conceptual framework. *Journal of Interdisciplinary Studies in Education*, 12(1), 23–43.

Yoon, B. (2021). English language learners' language and literacy development: A brief synopsis of major theoretical orientations for middle school teachers. *Middle School Journal*, 52(1), 23–29. https://doi.org/10.1080/00940771.2020.1840270

Yough, M., Slaten, C. D., Sankofa, N., Li, J., & Anderman, E. M. (2023). English language learner perceptions of school climate and teacher-student relationships: Role of acculturation and implications for achievement. Learning environments research: *An International Journal,* 1–18. https://doi.org/10.1007/s10984-023-09469-7

Zaidi, R., Oliver, C., Strong, T., & Alwarraq, H. (2021). Behind successful refugee parental engagement: The barriers and challenges. *Canadian Journal of Education,* 44(4), 907 937. https://doi.org/10.53967/cje-rce.v44i4.4537

Zakarneh, B. I., Alsalhi, N. R., Talab, A. R. A. B., Mansour, H. M., & Moh'd J Mahmoud, M. (2021). Social interactions as a barrier to second language learning: A sociocultural perspective. *International Journal of English Language and Literature Studies, 10*(2), 145-157.

Zeng, M., Wang, F., Xiang, S., Lin, B., Gao, C., & Li, J. (2020). Inheritance or variation? Spatial regeneration and acculturation via implantation of cultural and creative industries in Beijing's traditional compounds. *Habitat International,* 95, 102071.

Zhang, F., Shen, Y., Pasquarella, A., & Coker Jr., D. L. (2022). Early writing skills of English language learners (ELLs) and native English speakers (NESs): Examining predictors of contextualized spelling, writing fluency, and writing quality. *Reading & Writing,* 35(5), 1177–1200. https://doi.org/10.1007/s11145-021-10223-9

Hello!

My name is Edner Pierrevil, and I am a researcher and a doctoral candidate at the National University. I am conducting a research study on the acculturation experiences of ELLs within the classroom learning environment in the United States of America.

I am recruiting classroom teachers who meet all of these criteria:

1. Have experience working with ELLs in the Southeastern United States.
2. Have a current teaching license in the Southeastern United States.
3. Currently teaching at a public school in the Southeastern United States.

If you decide to participate in this study, you will be asked to do the following activities:

1. Create a pseudonym for yourself that will be used during the study.
2. Participate in Google Meet or face-to-face, 1:1 a 60–90-minute semi structured interview.
3. The interview will be scheduled at a time that is convenient to you and the researcher.
4. Google Meet is an online video conference platform.
5. There will be seventeen interview questions and possibly seven follow-up questions.
6. Respond to the demographic questions.
7. You will be asked to respond to questions about the acculturation experiences of ELLs within the classroom learning environment in the United States.
8. Participate in a 10-minute debrief after the interview for clarity, if needed.

9. Review your interview transcription within 72 hours after the interview to ensure the accuracy of your experiences with ELLs.

During these activities, you will be asked questions about:

- What are teachers' lived experiences of the acculturation faced by ELLs within the classroom learning environment in the United States?
- What are teachers' lived experiences addressing the acculturation experiences faced by ELLs within the classroom learning environment in the United States?
- What are strategies that teachers use to address the acculturation experiences of ELLs within the classroom learning environments in the United States?

Participants will receive $20 cash via email after the interview.

To participate or ask questions, please contact me at e.pierre vil7622@o365.ncu.edu.

Thank you for considering participating in this voluntary research!
Edner Pierrevil Researcher

**Interviewee's Name:**______ ____**Date** ____________-
**Time**________**Location**__________
   **Researcher's Name:** _____ ____**Date** ____________-
**Time**________**Location**__________

**Introduction**

Thank you for taking the time to meet with me today. How are you doing today? (The researcher is taking a moment to listen and connect with the participant). Well, let me introduce myself. I am Edner Pierrevil, a doctoral candidate at National University. I am conducting this research to explore the acculturation experiences of ELLs within the classroom learning environment in the United States of America.

# Demographic Questionnaire

1. How long have you been a teacher in Southeastern of the United States? ___
2. How many years have you been teaching ELLs? ________
3. What grades of ELLs do you have experience teaching or working? Prekindergarten____ Kindergarten_____1____ 2____ 3____ 4____ 5___
4. What grades of ELLs do you currently teach? Prekindergarten____ Kindergarten____ 1____ 2____ 3____ 4____ 5___and how many ELL students do you currently have in your classroom?______
5. What is your higher education?

   ________________________________________
6. What is your ethnic background?

   ______________________________________
7. What is your Gender? Male____________________Female___________ Other_______

**Clarification of terms will be used in this interview**

- Acculturation is defined as the acquisition of a new culture and assimilation to the new changes.
- Assimilation is referred to when an individual does not maintain his or her culture but adapts to the main culture.
- Classroom learning is a creative and critical environment that influences the student's academic achievement.
- English Language Learners (ELLs) are students whose English language is not their first language.
- Learning environment is a conducive classroom learning environment directly affects students' learning and development.

## Review the Informed Consent

First, before we begin the interview, I would like to review the informed consent, the demographic questionnaire, and the interview questions with you. (The researcher provides a copy of the consent, demographic questionnaire, and the interview questions to the participant). The researcher asks the following questions: "1. Do you have any questions about the informed consent or the interview questions? Yes__ No__ 2. Now, do you give me your consent to record this interview session yes__ No__?)." Thank you! Also, I want to let you know that your participation in this study is voluntary. You can withdraw or skip any question you do not want to answer. After the interview, you will receive a $20 incentive in cash.

## The Interview Session

Now, do you have any concerns or questions that I may need to clarify before we begin the interview session? I will ask you 17 questions related to the acculturation experience of ELLs. Also, I may ask you seven follow-up questions related to the research questions and the purpose of the study. Please feel comfortable while you are helping me explore the acculturation experiences of ELLs within the classroom learning environment in the United States of America. Okay, It is time to begin the interview! I am going to ask you the first question; please let me know when you are ready.

## The Interview Questions

RQ1. **What are teachers' lived experiences of the acculturation of ELLs within the classroom learning environment in the United States?**

1. Tell me about your experiences with ELLs in the United States.

2. How do teachers describe the acculturation experiences of ELLs within the classroom learning environment in the United States?

3. What challenges related to acculturation experiences do ELLs face in the classroom that you observe regularly?

4. Please describe to me what the acculturation lived experiences look like for ELLs.

5. How do you recognize when an ELL faces acculturation experiences in the classroom that differ from what native English speakers encounter?

6. Describe a situation where ELLs faced acculturation experiences, and what was the outcome of those lived experiences?

7. Based on your teacher experience, what have you observed as the cause of the ELLs' struggle to acculturate into the classroom learning environment?

8. Tell me how the acculturation experiences affected ELLs (academically) in the classrooms.

**RQ1. The Follow-up Interview Questions**

1. Can you describe an example of where ELLs were affected by these acculturation experiences in the school cultural environment?

2. Please describe to me why overcoming these acculturation experiences is uniquely crucial for ELLs.

3. How do you witness ELLs cope with the acculturation experiences in their classroom environments?

**RQ2. What are teachers' lived experiences addressing the acculturation of ELLs within the classroom learning environment in the United States?**

9. Describe for me what you do as a teacher to address the acculturation experiences of ELLs in your classroom.

10. What kind of cultural support do you provide to ELLs who face acculturation experiences in your classroom?

11. What meaning do you give to the acculturation experiences of ELLs in Southeastern?

**RQ2. The follow-Up Interview Questions**

1. Why is addressing these acculturation experiences essential for the population of ELLs?

2. How do acculturation experiences faced by ELLs affect their learning achievements as a population?

**RQ3. What are strategies that teachers use to address the acculturation experiences of ELLs within the classroom learning environments in the United States?**

12. What are the challenges teachers face in addressing the acculturation of ELLs within the classroom learning environment in the United States?

13. What are the acculturation strategies teachers use to address the acculturation experiences of ELLs?

14. How can ELLs overcome their acculturation experiences in the classroom learning environment?

15. In what ways do you help ELLs overcome their acculturation experiences?

16. How do ELLs respond when they successfully overcome their acculturation experiences?

17. Please describe how to meet the needs of ELLs who faced acculturation experiences in the classrooms.

**RQ3.The follow-Up Interview Questions**

1. What are the strategies teachers use to support the acculturation experiences of ELLs within the classroom learning environment?

2. How do ELLs cope with their acculturation experiences?

*Add. Is there anything else you would like to add?*

## Conclusion

Is there anything else you would like to add before we end this interview session? Thank you for your participation in this study. I will transcribe your interview within 24 hours. Then, I will email you a copy of your interview transcripts so members can check to see if I transcribed your interview correctly. Please let me know if you want to make any changes. Thank you for sharing your experiences with me during this interview, and have a great day.

Date: [ xx/xx/ 2023 date of permission]

Hello NU IRB,

My name is [name of permission granter], and I am [professional title] at [name of the school] School.

I have reviewed Edner Pierrevil's study, and I understand that he is recruiting participants who meet all of the following criteria:

The participants that will be in this study must meet the following criteria:

1. Have experience working with ELLs in the Southeastern United States.
2. Have a current teaching license in the Southeastern United States.
3. Currently teaching at a public school in the Southeastern United States.

I grant permission to Edner Pierrevil to do the following:

1. Obtain information to identify teachers who have experience working with ELLs.
2. Distribute the recruitment letter to potential participants through email and mailbox.
3. Conduct a Google Meet or face-to-face, 1:1 a 60–90-minute semi structured interview.
4. The interview will be scheduled at a time that is convenient for the participant and the researcher.
5. The participant will be asked seventeen interview questions, possibly seven follow-up questions, and demographic questions.

6.  The participant will be asked to respond to questions about the acculturation experiences of ELLs within the classroom learning environment in the United States.

If you have questions and would like to reach me, please contact me at [contact information for permission granter].

Thank you for your time,

[permission granter's full signature block with contact information]

# Introduction

My name is Edner Pierrevil, and I am a doctoral candidate at National University (NU). I am asking you to take part in a research study about the acculturation experiences of English Language Learners (ELLs) within the classroom learning environment in the United States of America. The name of the research study is "The acculturation experiences of ELLs within the classroom learning environment in the United States of America."

### *Eligibility*

You may participate in this research if you meet all of the following criteria:

1. Have experience working with ELLs in the Southeastern United States.
2. Have a current teaching license in the Southeastern United States.
3. Currently teaching at a public school in the Southeastern United States.

I hope to include 5-10 classroom teachers in this study.

**What you will be asked to do:** If you agree to participate in this study, you will be asked to do the following activities:

1. Create a pseudonym for yourself that will be used during the study.
2. Participate in Google Meet or face-to-face, 1:1 a 60–90-minute semi-structured interview.
3. The researcher will schedule the interview at a convenient time for you.
4. Google Meet is an online video conference platform.

5. There will be seventeenth interview questions and possibly seven follow-up questions.
6. Respond to the demographic questions.
7. You will be asked to respond to questions about the acculturation experiences of ELLs within the classroom learning environment in the United States.
8. Participate in a 10-minute debrief after the interview for clarity, if needed.
9. Review your interview transcription via email within 72 hours after the interview to ensure the accuracy of your experiences with ELLs.

### *Risks*

There are no foreseeable risks or discomforts directly associated with this study. However, the participants may feel discomfort when discussing their lived experiences with ELLs. To minimize any risks and discomfort that may arise, you can skip any question you do not wish to answer or skip any activity. Also, you can stop participating at any time without any penalty.

### *Benefits*

There is no direct benefit for participants in this study. This research may contribute to the body of knowledge in the subject area of this study.

### *Privacy and Data Protection*

The researcher of this study will not link the data to the participants of this study. The data will not include information that can identify your name, address, etc.

The researcher will protect and secure all your personal information, but I

cannot guarantee the confidentiality of your research data. In addition to me, the following people

and offices will have access to your data:

- My NU dissertation committee and any appropriate NU support or leadership staff
- The NU Institutional Review Board

This data could be used for future research studies or distributed to other investigators for future

research studies without additional informed consent from you or your legally authorized

representative.

### *How the Results Will Be Used*

I will publish the results in a dissertation format. The researcher may also share the results in a presentation or publication. Participants will not be identified in the results.

### *Compensation*

After you complete the interview, you will receive a $20 Cash or Zelle.

**Confidentiality:** I will keep records of this study private and take reasonable measures to protect the security of all your personal information. In any report I make public, I will not include any information that will make it possible to identify you. I will securely store your data for three years. Then, I will delete electronic data and destroy paper data.

### **Taking part is voluntary**

Participation in this study is entirely voluntary. You may quit at any time.

**If you have questions**

Please ask any questions you have now. If you have questions later, please contact me at e.pierrevil7622@o365.ncu.edu or (561)729-3334.

If you have any questions or concerns regarding your rights as a subject in this study, you may contact the Institutional Review Board (IRB) via email at irb@nu.edu

# Appendix E IRB Approval



**IRB-FY23-24-687 - Initial: Exempt from Further Review**

do-not-reply@cayuse.com <do-not-reply@cayuse.com>
Tue 1/16/2024 9:35 PM
To dverace@ncu.edu <dverace@ncu.edu>,Edner Pierrevil <E.Pierrevil7622@o365.ncu.edu>

**National**
UNIVERSITY

**9388 Lightwave Ave.**
**San Diego, CA 92123**
**irb@nu.edu**

**Notice of Exemption**

January 16, 2024

**To:** Edner Pierrevil

**Project Title:** The Acculturation Experiences of ELLs Within the Classroom Learning Environment in the United States of America
**NU IRB Number:** IRB-FY23-24-687
**Determination:** Exempt from further review 45 CFR 46.101 Category 2 (ii). Research that only includes interactions involving educational tests (cognitive, diagnostic, aptitude, achievement), survey procedures, interview procedures, or observation of public behavior (including visual or auditory recording) if at least one of the following criteria is met:
Any disclosure of the human subjects' responses outside the research would not reasonably place the subjects at risk of criminal or civil liability or be damaging to the subjects' financial standing, employability, educational advancement, or reputation; or

**Status: Active - Research activities may begin as of January 16, 2024**

Dear Edner Pierrevil:

The study referenced above has been reviewed by the National University IRB. The IRB has determined your research is exempt from further review under 45 CFR 46.104, which means you will not need to renew your study and may begin your study effective immediately. However, if you find the need to change your study in any way, you will need to submit a modification to the IRB prior to implementing the changes. This will allow the IRB to determine whether or not the study still meets exemption criteria.



Sincerely,

Dr. Joseph Marron, IRB Chair

Dr. Brianne Mongeon, Director, HRPP & IRB

Jenessa Eberhardt, Associate Director, HRPP & IRB

Dear [Recipient's Name],

I hope this message finds you well. My name is Edner Pierrevil, and I am a doctoral candidate at National University. I am currently in the midst of an important research study titled "The Acculturation Experiences of ELLs Within the Classroom Learning Environment in the United States." This study is now entering its field-testing phase, and your expertise in qualitative research and experience with ELLs (English Language Learners) makes you an ideal candidate for providing invaluable insights.

The primary aim of involving field-testing experts like yourself is to ensure that the interview questions are meticulously aligned with the research questions. This alignment is crucial for generating meaningful data for the study. Your feedback will significantly contribute to the credibility and trustworthiness of this qualitative descriptive phenomenological study.

Should you choose to participate, your role will involve reviewing the interview questions and providing feedback on their suitability to meet the study's objectives. Your expert opinion will be highly valued in enhancing the appropriateness of these questions. Additionally, your participation will be acknowledged in the dissertation's appendix, where your name and qualifications will be listed to underscore the study's integrity.

If you are willing to contribute to this endeavor, please respond to this email by [date] to confirm your participation. Upon your confirmation, I will forward you the interview questions along with the research questions and the study's purpose for your review.

For any further clarification or if you wish to discuss this in more detail, please feel free to contact me at (561)-729-3334 or e.pierre vil7622@o365.ncu.edu. Your expertise and time are greatly appreciated, and I look forward to the possibility of your valuable contribution to this study.

Sincerely,
Edner Pierrevil
Doctoral Candidate
National University

Dr. C.B. has ten years of experience as a certified school counselor and six years as a middle school counselor. Also, she has a Master of Science in counseling psychology (School Counseling and Mental Health tracks) and a doctorate in Educational Leadership. She believed that the interview guide was suitable to explore the acculturation experiences faced by ELLs within the classroom learning environment. The second expert was Dr. Charlene Desir, a qualitative research professor at Nova Southeastern University (NSU). She has an Ed.D. from Harvard and an Advanced Certificate in Qualitative Methods from Nova Southeastern University. She provided several suggestions that were implemented and contributed to making the interview guide suitable to meet the purpose of the study. For instance, she suggested focusing on teachers' experiences that support the acculturation of ELLs in the classroom in the United States and the meaning of the teachers witnessing the acculturation experiences of ELLs. The third expert was Dr. Vardine Simeus; she has a Ph.D. and 22 years of experience as a Clinical Director, Adjunct Professor, Owner of Safe Landing Consulting, LLC, Director of Social Emotional Wellness in Schools and Aftercare Programs, and Psychotherapist. She stated that the questions engage the participants in conducting a phenomenological study. All the experts have experience working with the population of ELLs in the southeastern United States.

**Acculturate**: to learn to live successfully in a different culture

**Acculturation:** the process of learning to live successfully in a different culture.

**Assimilate:** something to fully understand an idea or some information so that you are able to use it yourself.

**Acquisition:** the process of gradually learning something or gaining something such as a skill. Bilingual acquisition occurs in different socio-cultural contexts, and it entails different language combinations and modalities.

**Assimilation:** the process of fully understanding an idea or some information so that you are able to use it yourself.

**Awareness:** knowledge that something exists or understanding of a situation or subject at the present time based on information or experience. Public awareness of the problem will make politicians take it seriously.

**Bilingual:** able to use two languages equally well. Bilingual education includes a variety of strategies for using a student's native language in addition to English.

**Classroom**: a room in a school or college where groups of students are taught. In what ways do learners and teachers participate in language classroom activity?

**Culture:** the customs and beliefs, art, way of life and social organization of a particular country or group.

**Cultural:** connected with the culture of a particular society or group, its customs, beliefs,

**Culturally:** in a way that is connected with the culture of particular societies or groups, their customs, beliefs, etc.

**Diverse:** including many different types of people or things. Miami is a very culturally diverse city.

**Diversity:** the fact of many different types of things or people being included in something; a range of different things or people. She teaches the students to have respect for different races and appreciate the diversity of other cultures.

**Environment:** the conditions that you live or work in and the way that they influence how you feel or how effectively you can work. A learning/working environment

**Inclusion:** the act of including someone or something as part of a group, list, etc., or a person or thing that is included. The idea is that everyone should be able to use the same facilities, take part in the same activities, and enjoy the same experiences, including people who have a disability or other disadvantages. The act of allowing many different types of people to do something and treating them fairly and equally.

**Immigrant:** a person who has come to live permanently in a different country from the one they were born in.

**Integrate:** to become or make somebody become accepted as a member of a social group, especially when they come from a different culture. They have not made any effort to integrate with the local community.

**Integration:** the act or process of combining two or more things so that they work together. The act or process of mixing people who have previously been separated, usually because of culture, color, race, religion, etc.

**Language:** a system of communication consisting of sounds, words, and grammar. She does research into how children acquire language. A system of communication used by people living in a particular country: Do you speak any foreign languages? Too many children leave school with poor language skills, and are unable to compose a letter or email.

**Learning:** the activity of obtaining knowledge. The process of getting an understanding of something by studying it or by experience. Knowledge and learning are essential factors for achieving successful outcomes. Some students have a more analytical approach to learning. The idea with young children is to integrate learning with play.

**Marginalization:** the process or result of making somebody feel as if they are not important and cannot influence decisions or events; the fact of putting somebody in a position in which they have no power.

**Separate:** forming a unit by itself, not joined to something else. The school is housed in two separate buildings.

**Separation:** the act of separating people or things; the state of being separate.

https://dictionary.cambridge.org/us/dictionary